The Analysis of FAILURE

The Analysis of FAILURE

An Investigation of Failed Cases in Psychoanalysis and Psychotherapy

Arnold Goldberg

Routledge
Taylor & Francis Group

New York   London

Routledge
Taylor & Francis Group
711 Third Avenue
New York, NY 10017

Routledge
Taylor & Francis Group
27 Church Road
Hove, East Sussex BN3 2FA

Printed in the United States of America on acid-free paper
10 9 8 7 6 5 4 3 2 1

International Standard Book Number: 978-0-415-89302-2 (Hardback) 978-0-415-89303-9 (Paperback)

Library of Congress Cataloging-in-Publication Data

Goldberg, Arnold, 1929-
    The analysis of failure : an investigation of failed cases in psychoanalysis and psychotherapy / Arnold I. Goldberg.
        p. cm.
    Includes bibliographical references and index.
        ISBN 978-0-415-89302-2 (hbk. : alk. paper) -- ISBN 978-0-415-89303-9 (pbk. : alk. paper) -- ISBN 978-0-203-81710-0 (e-book)
        1. Psychotherapy--Evaluation. 2. Psychoanalysis--Evaluation. 3. Psychotherapist and patient. I. Title.

RC480.5.G583 2012
616.89'14--dc22
                                                                            2011008125

Visit the Taylor & Francis Web site at
http://www.taylorandfrancis.com

and the Routledge Web site at
http://www.routledgementalhealth.com

To Connie, Sarah, and Andrew

Contents

Acknowledgments

This book grew out of a seminar at the Institute for Psycho-analysis of Chicago on failed cases. I am grateful to the analysts and analytic candidates and others who attended the seminar and especially to those who remained with us throughout its entire existence. I am especially indebted to those who volunteered to present their cases of failure to our seminar. I wish I could list all the names of the attendees and presenters, but it is probably prudent for them to remain confidential. The patients mentioned in the book have all been disguised or are composite patients that were constructed from a wide number of sources, so confidentiality prohibits much more than an overall message of gratitude. Finally, I am surprised to realize that I am also grateful to those who were too reluctant and/or frightened to present and so came up with a variety of excuses. They allowed for a better understanding of what failure means to us and does to us all. I hope the reader shares in my gratitude.

Thanks to Dr. William Scheftner, chair of the Department of Psychiatry at Rush University Medical Center, and the Michael Franz Basch Research Fund for financial support; to Denise Duval and Dennis Shelby for their help with the statistics; and to my secretary Christine Susman.

1

Introducing Failure
Who's the Greatest?

A friend once told me that, although he was an outstanding violinist, he had decided to pursue a career in medicine rather than the promise of a concert career when he realized that he would never be one of the world's five or ten greatest violinists. So, too, had a brilliant PhD in philosophy decided to become a psychologist because, in her words, there was "only one Kant." There are surely a number of reasons for a hope for fulfillment in one field of endeavor becoming diverted or compromised, but a good number of these changes in direction do involve a modification or a redeployment of what many psychoanalysts consider to be a driving force of ambition: a grandiose fantasy. First explained, developed, and investigated by Heinz Kohut, the attribution of feelings of specialness and greatness was examined in the infantile exhibitionism and associated responsiveness of mirroring in the caretaking mother (Kohut, 1971). The later expression of this infantile grandiosity was noted in flying fantasies along with the concomitant excitement of such a psychological display.

If one follows the progress of infantile grandiosity, it is usually manifested in a variety of displays of exhibitionism and personal specialness along with its beginning transformation into the more or less acceptable forms of personal ambition. Although it may be felt that the grandiose exhibitionistic fantasies of infancy are universal, the ultimate fate of these central forces is both complex and problematic. Initially one might feel the possibilities for the eventual resting place for grandiose fantasies are infinite, but it may well be possible to study the varieties of deployment of a personal feeling of importance, significance, and even greatness.

From the complete repression of the aforementioned fantasy, to the preconscious and even conscious suppression of it, to the more open and even naked display of the derivatives of grandiosity and ambition, it may be equally plausible to correlate some developmental experience to the later expression of the alterations and modifications of this fantasy that is enjoyed by some and despised by others. Everything from birth order to all of the vicissitudes of early childhood becomes relevant to the emergence and persistence of the derivatives and alterations of one's exhibitionism and grandiosity. Perhaps no more common and recognizable than any is the rescue fantasy.

From the Lone Ranger to Superman, our childhood heroes are those who rescue and save the unfortunate. Whether those needing rescue are miners trapped underground or last-minute, coming-from-behind, winning athletic teams, we are uniformly excited by the rescue process. Just as blatant exhibitionism or naked ambition is to be shunned and condemned, rescues are uniformly admirable. Indeed, often the ideal hero is one who is humble in the midst of applause. Our society makes a virtue of this particular derivative of the wish to be great, and there is no more poignant image than that of the person rushing into a burning building to save a child while oblivious to his or her own personal danger. And so, not surprisingly, there is no more painful tale than that of a rescue that falls on its face. Failure lurks in the shadows of every rescue attempt, and the fantasy that accompanies every rescue is haunted by the ease in which it may lead to jeers instead of cheers.

It is no surprise to realize our recognition of the essence of failure as the destruction of our need to rescue and to achieve fulfillment of our earliest wish for admiration. We hate failure not only for the obvious but also for what it does to our self-esteem. It is probably not far afield to conclude that our violinist and philosopher managed to channel their wish to be the greatest into a life of rescuing.

By no means should the practice of psychoanalysis and psychotherapy be limited to or reduced to the mere expression of our rescue fantasies, but it is an interesting exercise to observe the sometimes intense emotions that accompany success or failure in the light of this element of unconscious motivation. This is especially true when one studies how such strong feelings may inhibit a more objective study of failure.

FAILURE AND PROMISE

It has always seemed to me that the familiar childhood guide to living, "If at first you don't succeed, try, try again" was not advising mere repetition, but rather it implied that one should modify one's effort by trying harder, doing something else, or doing whatever quite differently. That is not exactly what seems to be the guiding theme in the literature on success or failure in psychoanalysis and psychotherapy. We do, however, recognize that these two words—success or failure—allow all sorts of gradations in between. One may fail to become a concert pianist or to be fluent in French yet be able to adequately play a few tunes and/or perhaps to order dinner in a bistro. There are failures that merely mean falling short. We also recognize that one may simply not be cut out for a particular endeavor, and the piano or that particular language may just not be your cup of tea. One would do well to pursue the clarinet or give German a try. This latter suggestion is also not much of a theme in the literature on success or failure in psychoanalysis. Much more emphasized are the mistakes made, the errors committed, and the problems that can be corrected. Associated with this aura of wrongdoing is the feeling of shame or humiliation as if one were clearly to blame for the failure, a sentiment that rarely accompanies a wipeout in the piano or clarinet.

Along with the fact of failure and its accompanying effect of either shame or remorse is another state of mind that serves to distinguish some failures from others, and that is the movement toward correction. When I failed to develop as a great clarinet player, there was but a mild feeling of regret and absolutely no feeling consisting of an urge to correct my mistakes. I could readily abandon that instrument with a mere shrug of having tried and failed. Bad luck! This degree of concern or lack of concern is the hallmark for the assignment of blame or responsibility, a state closely allied with success or failure but at times easily placed on the shoulders of fate, talent, or mere happenstance. I could be a dud at the clarinet through no fault of my own. I was not to blame. All that was required was the trying, and I need not try, try again.

To properly position success or failure in the arena of psychoanalysis and psychotherapy, one must also tackle the issue of promise. The word *promise* is as ambiguous as many in our language, but we shall restrict it to its meaning in a relationship in which one is promised something by another. It is a relationship defined by my dictionary as "a declaration of assurance by which a person undertakes a commitment to do or refrain from doing a specific act or guarantees that a specific thing will or will not happen, be done."

It takes no psychoanalytic wizardry to see this as a typical parent–child relationship with its overtones of trust and disappointment. One person is in a position of power, and one in a position of submission. However, the psychoanalyst sees this relationship also as a carrier of transference in which one person is idealized and admired by another. The assignment of this idealization enables the process of treatment to continue, and the failure of this idealization leads to a disappointment that may be severe and even intractable. The therapist is accordingly the bearer of one form of rescue fantasy that is fueled by an associated grandiose fantasy of cure. This is especially the case if one is called upon to treat a patient who has not been well served by a previous therapist. The grandiosity is often coupled with a variety of exhibitionist fantasies as well. Surely all of medicine, psychiatry, psychoanalysis, and psychotherapy are filled with promise and equally concerned with failure and disappointment. It is thus to be expected that our time and energy will be filled with fulfilling promises and banishing disappointments. It may sound perverse to investigate failure as anything other than an absence or deficiency. It may seem outrageous to afford failure a status in its own right, just as it is ridiculous to see a bad parent as anything other than one missing the traits accorded to good parenting.

And yet if we carry the analogy further, we can easily recognize the glow of satisfaction as a parent details the accomplishments of his or her offspring, and the lack of any clear stance to take as a parent may reflect the sad state of affairs in one or more children. Sometimes we sympathize, sometimes we secretly or not so secretly blame, and sometimes we advise. The happy parent ordinarily takes a good deal of credit. The unhappy parent is often left to struggle with responsibility. He or she has a continuum of possible positions ranging from "It was all my fault; I failed as a parent," to "These things just happen, and no one is to blame," to a variant of "He fell into bad company" or "It was the drugs." The psychoanalyst arrives on the scene in an effort to untangle the unconscious elements in each of these positions. You may glow when your child graduates from college or wins first place in a race, but the assignment of credit may be problematic. You may be despondent when your child drops out of college or comes in out of the running in a race, but the assignment of blame is equally dubious. Of course, we should be equally uncertain about success or failure in psychoanalysis or psychotherapy, but we are rarely able to maintain objectivity in these enterprises. That is the point in an analysis of failure.

Without getting too deeply into philosophy, it is fair to say that we have learned from Friedrich Nietzsche, Ferdinand de Saussure, and Claude Levi-Strauss that our language, our thinking, and our social institutions are organized on the basis of oppositions: true and false, inside and outside, appearance and reality, man and woman. No better binary set exists than that of failure and success. Although philosophers such as Jacques Derrida have made much of the inherent contradictions in our language (Delacampagne, 1999) in the popularity of deconstruction (see Chapter 5), today we all agree that the existing culture determines how we consider these binary oppositions, and so what constitutes success and what makes for failure are never exact issues in reality, but rather are decisions reached by the existing community of like-minded language users. This is no more than to say that there are no absolute conditions that determine a success or a failure; rather, they are subject to a series of rules, normative practices, opinions, and possibilities. Often there are stark and unarguable manifestations of success or failure, but frequently the decisions about success and failure are relative and changeable.

As difficult as it may seem, an effort must be made to understand failure in terms of its origins and its effects without allowing the moral and judgmental interferences and their associated feelings to intrude upon such a study. This is not to reduce it entirely to its possible unconscious origins any more than it is to dismiss these roots. It is quite difficult to divorce such an emotionally loaded concept from these accompanying effects, and so the fate of failure has been that of similarly experienced terms such as those commonly confronted in boundary violations. The kneejerk reaction to all forms of misbehavior on the part of an analyst or therapist is one of condemnation based on a template of propriety and moral correctness. Failure is rather quickly assigned to the category of having done something wrong, and so it cannot escape having the cloud of error interfere with an investigation that is in need of objectivity. A similar lack of objectivity may be found in the myriad of reports of successful cases. A moral judgment should have no place in these assessments (Goldberg, 2007), but this is not a plea for its banishment but one for understanding how we feel about both success and failure in their own right.

We must see failure and success as belonging to the realm of polysemy (i.e., words that can have many meanings). They can mean one thing in one sentence and something different in another. And they can mean one thing to one person and quite a different thing to another. To add to the complexity of determining just what failure and success mean, we must reckon with the present state of pluralism in psychoanalysis and psychotherapy. We live in a world of diverse theoretical systems that organize clinical data according to ego psychology, object relations, self psychology, or any other theoretical structure. Inasmuch as our theoretical eyes focus on one part of a set of clinical data rather than another, our adherence to any particular theory naturally limits what we observe. All in all, there can be no guarantee that agreement on the failure or success of any single case will be clear-cut and unanimous. The popularity of a neuroscientific approach to mental maladies holds out the promise of a neat cause-and-effect way of evaluating success or failure, but the interpretive or hermeneutic basis of analysis and therapy belies that promise. Our material is ever subject to an evaluative process that goes beyond the obvious to factors beneath the surface.

We have also noted the moral overtones to any inquiry about failure, which includes a number of key concepts including *ought, should, must, good, bad, right*, and *wrong*. Some authors (Thompson, 2010) have tried to move our concern with the "normative" aspect of things such as we find in medicine's preoccupation with normal weight or ideal blood pressure or in legal concerns with boundary violations or ethical lapses over to a study of normativity per se. Various normative concerns can be divided into two key concepts, consisting of those involving evaluations and those that involve directives. Evaluations assess the way things are or might be as good or as bad, as desirable or otherwise. Directives tell one how to behave or think. In contrast to good or bad, we have key notions involving what one ought to do or should do. We might fold a hand in a poker game without any question of morality. In different areas, the evaluations hold priority over the directives, whereas the reverse may be true in other areas. Too often we find ethical issues hold sway over these decisions. However, there is often a voice for a form of behavior that triumphs over the moral or ethical, and we shall see that this dilemma is not uncommon in failed cases. The right thing to do has its own normative scale, and this does not always coincide with the best thing to do.

A very common comment after hearing a case presentation of failure has to do with what one ought to have done. However, an equally common comment may well be one stating what one ought not to have done. There is no denying that we, for the most part, are engaged in an activity that consists of following a certain set of rules established by a certain authority or a system of behavior that is rooted in a set of principles. These principles carry the aura of correctness, and defying them is seen as a mistake. But all mistakes need not lead to failures, because some succeed. In those cases, what we ought to have done may not be for the best, and our oughts and our principles can be seen as but a matter of shared ideas rather than fundamental truths.

The literature on failure inevitably avoids an endpoint of resignation and usually reports how errors were undone and success was finally achieved. Failure is banished, and any investigation of failure seems to automatically assume that an error was responsible. Yet in spite of the seeming correctness of that stance, it does seem possible to analyze failure in its own right. We already do some of that in our recognition of a propensity in some patients to "need to fail." We also extend that idea in the further recognition of some patients' need or wish to have their analyst or therapist fail. We also embrace the fact that it may be therapeutic for a patient who is overly grandiose to experience failure. All sorts of possibilities may present themselves if we allow ourselves the opportunity to contemplate failure without the opprobrium usually attached to the word. That is what an analysis of failure is all about.

TAKING SIDES

One way to visualize or perhaps to dramatize the usual unfolding of a therapeutic process is that of considering the therapist, be it a psychiatrist, psychotherapist, or psychoanalyst, as allied with the patient against the problem or symptoms of the patient. Over time the patient in analysis becomes aware of the unconscious contributions to the problems, and he or she struggles in an adversarial relationship with what has been previously unknown and unacknowledged. Just as the psychiatrist joins with the patient by way of medication to fight an illness that is seen as something to be rid of, so too is any psychological intervention similarly characterized. As the contest of this hoped-for elimination proceeds, the aim of the patient and therapist is that the alliance becomes strengthened and the illness ultimately is vanquished or at least is neutralized and managed. Failure is different. The illness remains, and the alliance is strained. To be sure, a number of therapists remain supportive and sympathetic to their unhelped patients, but a surprisingly large number become antagonistic toward the patient, especially if the patient has departed with his or her illness intact and unchanged. The fall from the position of power or wisdom that the unsuccessful analyst or therapist must experience and endure is often accompanied by rage associated with the narcissistic injury that marks the impotence of the therapist. The anger that was directed at the illness may become directed at the patient in the form of disparaging his or her lack of cooperation, lack of effort, need to be sick, or a variety of other calumnies of blame and/or ridicule. The therapist or analyst has moved from ally to antagonist toward the patient in order to handle the hurt of failure. What follows is an opportunity to allow some of these feelings to emerge.

The recurrent theme that will present itself is that of properly positioning failure. Is it the fault of the patient or the therapist, or does it belong to both? Is it mutually constructed, or does it inevitably emerge no matter who attempts to deal with it? Situating failure is, of course, a move to place blame and responsibility and so may make it even more difficult to understand it. We shall see the efforts that are made to avoid the topic with the faint hope that perhaps one day the entire preoccupation with it will merely disappear.

At the end of an analysis, a grateful patient turns to the analyst and thanks him or her for all that has been accomplished. The analyst assures the patient that the achievement is to be shared, but the patient insists that all of the success is due to the analyst's efforts. Another analytic patient has decided to end an analysis with the sad decision that nothing has been accomplished, and there is no need to waste more time and money. The patient says that perhaps he or she is just not cut out for analysis, but the unspoken message is that of a failure laid at the feet of the analyst. That is the most common scenario, followed by some soul searching by the analyst who often can go no further in determining just what went wrong. Until the feelings are recognized and their meanings understood, failure will remain as the dirt swept under the carpet.

Let us begin with a review of some authors who have written on the subject.

AN OVERVIEW OF THE LITERATURE ON FAILURE

Although there may be more of a concentration in the literature on the positive and ameliorative effects of both psychoanalytic and psychotherapeutic activity for patients (Shedler, 2010), the acknowledgment of both the failure (Chessick, 1996) along with the harmful effects of treatment (Barlow, 2010) has not gone unnoticed and unexamined. However, the more common approach to problematic cases is to investigate the nature of the difficulty as something that can be removed, overcome, or found to lie outside of the method that is being employed. Therefore an impasse or a failure, much as a disease or even a developmental impediment, is seen as a hurdle to be overcome rather than an immovable obstacle to one's efforts. Thus the spirit of positive thinking reigns in the very way we think about failure. This, of course, is to be expected, and in no way should this be seen as a criticism of these efforts. However, it is possible that a more neutral position with the undertone of a proper and normative vision may reveal a different take on failure.

If we start with a rather common and popular view of failure, a convenient and easy definition is offered in a self-help book titled *The Joy of Success* (Collins, 2003), where failure is "simply incompletion, the inability to either complete or delete." The author went on to explain that people fail for different reasons such as lack of skill, unwillingness to ask, and saying yes when they should have said no. This approach considers failure solely as the negative of success with no attributes of its own. Yet one can also say that failure results at times from the very opposite, as in saying no when one should have said yes; from a rush to ask; and even from being overly skillful and doing more than is necessary. Hearts fail from a muscular weakness but also from overexcitement; computers crash from insufficient information as well as from excessive demand. One can spin the cause according to one's preferences, and no light is shed with statements that begin, "Failure is simply _____." Failure is complicated. Especially in psychotherapy, it is multidimensional and in need of more careful analysis.

Perhaps the most extreme and even "wonderful" way to handle the issue of failure is that offered in the Rippen and Schulman (2003) book on failure in which M. Hyman (2003) said failure is an oxymoron, and the efficacy of the treatment is but another point to be analyzed. Of course, that very conclusion of failure as self-contradictory can itself serve as yet another point to be analyzed, and this relentless pursuit of the lack of finality may never come to rest. Donald Spence, in a panel on failure (Wallerstein & Coen, 1994), moved in a somewhat opposite direction by urging us to gather a literature on failure and so to collect a compendium of its causes and types. These opposing views between dodging the bullet and biting the bullet seem so to characterize the literature on failure that it is not surprising that a more comfortable middle ground has arisen, and that is in the concentration on the word and concept of *impasse*.

Although impasse warrants further discussion, it is noteworthy in the psychoanalytic and psychotherapeutic literature as being a far more popular concept than outright failure. Gedo and Gehrie (1993) saw it as a spur to innovation, whereas Wallerstein and Coen (1994) classified three kinds of impasses. The first consists of acting out, which impedes the progress of the analysis; the second is the negative therapeutic reaction; and the third is termed *anti-insight.* In an effort to differentiate an impasse from a failure, Chessick (1996) presented a clinical case that ends on an unsatisfactory note, which in turn led Chessick to introduce the concept of stalemate: A state that impedes progress best seems to allow further hope (i.e., neither an impasse nor a total bust).

Once the stop is made to grapple with failure per se, there is some confluence of opinion as to its value. Benjamin (2009) felt it important for analysts to regularly consider their personal feeling of failure while conducting an analysis in order to recover from the ruptures that occur in the course of the analysis. For Benjamin, failure is an ongoing part of every analysis. Judith Vida (2003), in the aforementioned Rippen and Schulman (2003) collection, said that failure is necessary in order for a therapist to grow. One may question this particular use of the word *failure* inasmuch as it flirts with ideas offered by Gedo and Gehrie that portray impasse as a spur to innovation. Again, the issue of finality presents itself in order to distinguish those failures on the road to success from object failures. The embrace of honest-to-goodness failure is discussed by Wolman (1972), Hoch (1948), and Rosenblum (1994) in descriptions ranging from patients who are unanalyzable to resistances that do not yield to interpretations. The struggle to properly position or situate a failure is seen in the range of opinions as to whether the failure is due to a patient who needs to fail (Fried,

1954), due to the limitations of the technique and process (Rippen & Schulman, 2003), or due to the very idea of untreatability.

An overview of the literature on failure and the related terms of *stalemate* and *impasse* reveals a few salient points. The first is that with a few exceptions (and there are exceptions to everything that can be said about failure), most analysts and therapists avoid discussing what it does and means to them and make great efforts to make lemonade from a bunch of lemons. We either deny the very existence of failure or dismiss it. Clearly the shame and humiliation of failure have inhibited its objective study. The second conclusion about what has been written about failure is its slipperiness. We shall later discuss how the words *failure* and *success* are representative of what is essentially a linguistic problem. Outside of suicides that succeed, there is not much in the conduct of psychoanalysis and psychotherapy that lends itself to clear-cut decisions about what qualifies as a bona fide failure, and outside of "living happily ever after" there is even less that is a sure sign of success. It is probably incorrect to call failure an oxymoron inasmuch as it is not really self-contradictory but more properly belongs to what is best termed an *undecidable*.

The third possible conclusion that may follow from our relative neglect of the subject (again with the exceptions noted) has been that of not better defining and determining the limitations of our particular theories and techniques. The incredible insularity of our various "schools" and "allegiances" has prevented the development of a fairly simple set of guidelines as to what works best for what. Every new idea spawns an excitement that unfortunately becomes joined with an exclusivity. Not every idea works for everything, and a proper study of failure and failures should ultimately enable us to make more reasonable and feasible applications of our particular modes of therapy.

The analysis of failure is best approached with the account of Humpty Dumpty in Lewis Carroll's *Through the Looking Glass* (1896/1982). It reads,

> "When I use a word," Humpty Dumpty said, in rather a scorned tone, "it means just what I choose it to mean—neither more nor less" … "The question is," said Alice, "whether you can make words mean so many different things" … "The question is," said Humpty Dumpty, "which is to be master—that's all." (p. 184)

Alice doesn't reply, so Humpty Dumpty continues, "They've a temper, some of them, particularly verbs: they're the proudest—adjectives you can do anything with but not verbs—however, I can manage the whole lot of them. Impenetrability! That's what I say" (p. 184).

In the true spirit of Humpty Dumpty, we shall proceed to see if we can master the impenetrability of a noun: *failure.*

2

The Failure Project

Some time ago, a colleague asked a study group that I attended the question of why people always presented cases that went well or had a minor problem and not cases that utterly failed. Of course, no one could easily answer that, because a reply would run the danger of having to do that very task (i.e., present a failed case). Once that hurdle had been overcome, a whole new set of problems would arise that ranged from studying why such presentations were constantly avoided to investigating both the nature and probable and possible causes of failure. Perhaps the very first discovery that one makes in pursuing such an investigation is that just about everyone has an opinion about failure, or, more accurately, a set of opinions. Usually these opinions are based upon one or possibly more personal experiences and might be more properly called *prejudices*. The next likely discovery is one that I personally learned only after submitting several papers about failure to several of our most prominent journals. That discovery is again best considered in the category of prejudice, and in its simplest form it is the advice given as to how to conduct a study of failed cases. This advice was usually delivered in very somber and sober tones with an occasional reference to Karl Popper, empirical research, or Thomas Kuhn. The adjectives that one might accurately attach to the advice ranged from *hilarious* to *impossible*. My very favorite was the one that suggested or urged me to abandon the study of cases that *had* failed to ones that *would* fail. This surely would necessitate examining a number of cases from their onset until they may or may not fail. Of course, one might spend many hours in pursuit of countless cases with no chance of stumbling across a failed case. The advice was offered in the most encouraging manner, stating that mine was a retrospective study (i.e., one that examined the failure after the fact) and should be more of a prospective one (i.e., one that saw failure unfold before it happened). Our sage offered no hint as to how to divine such occurrences but did urge me to start with a set of principles of success and wait until one or more were missing and so resulting in failure.

Unable to preselect cases of failure, we had to go ahead with a study of those cases declared to be failures by the psychoanalyst or psychotherapist who conducted the treatment.* That became a crucial issue in the gathering up of cases that failed or inasmuch as not everyone agreed on exactly what constituted failure. Another reader, from another journal rejecting another paper, informed us that there was a vast literature on the subject from other schools or therapists inspired by different theoretical approaches that called these cases "impasses" rather than failures. As previously noted, it would appear that the word *impasse* suggests a temporary problem that could be resolved by some other effort. The dictionary equates *impasse* with *blind alley* or *deadlock*, words that tend to create a possibility of solution if only one tries again in some new manner. *Failure* is not meant to be a word such as *impasse*, which lacks finality, because it is an endpoint that is not ordinarily modified as a temporary setback or an unfortunate start. Yet the readers (and there were several) appeared reluctant to assign such finality to the idea. Lurking in their judgment was a hidden appraisal so common to the very idea of failure (i.e., a mistake was made that could be repaired or undone). For some, all failures

---

* The treatments to be presented are either conducted by a psychotherapist or psychoanalyst and the reader should note that these categories are used interchangeably without a clear distinction in order to assure confidentiality.

were tentative and certainly no cases were beyond salvage. Hope must be kept alive.

Gathering up a group of failed cases despite the inherent vagueness of the concept gives way to the next question, "Why did it fail?" (i.e., what was the cause or causes?). There is a temptation to leave that question to the side while listening to the presentations of a number of cases in the hope that something will emerge that is the answer. Of course, we have learned that we always listen with some theory in mind, and so we attempted to isolate our preconceptions about failure to see if we could discover and defend them.

By way of summary, our project consisted of a group of analysts, analytic candidates, and psychotherapists listening to case presentations considered to be failures by the presenting analyst or therapist. Each case was graded as to its being a success or failure by the listeners who considered the case on the basis of both objective factors, such as the ability to work or get married or the removal or amelioration of a symptom, and subjective factors such as a feeling of well-being. Both therapist and patient were graded on these issues. We then attempted to evaluate the cases with regard to the cause of the failure on consideration of a number of factors, including a lack of knowledge on the therapist's part, a lack of an empathic connection, an inability to sustain empathy, and a failure to consider alternate approaches to treatment. Each of these possible reasons for a case failure was then examined as to whether or not a change in any of the reasons for the failure would have made a difference. One would think that there might be a correlation between the cause of the failure and the remedy; this did not seem to hold true and so underscored a general feeling of befuddlement amongst many of our listening judges, who so struggled with the idea of failure and the accompanying idea of an untreatable case. It would seem to be a logical conclusion that if a case failed in one's opinion because of a countertransference problem, then a correction of that problem would alleviate the failure. Not so. One is left much as we began. The case failed because of a countertransference problem, a lack of knowledge, or any imaginable reason, but it still might have failed even if that deficiency were corrected. Perhaps failure is a result of many factors.

THE CAUSES

The first category that was considered as a cause of failure was a simple lack of knowledge of what to do for and with a particular patient. I suspect this form of evaluation was extremely dependent on the listening audience, because a group of fairly well-trained analytic candidates and analysts rarely mentioned this deficiency of information as a significant factor in their evaluation of failure. This particular feature must initially be divided into two large sectors: The first asks if the person is knowledgeable about what he or she is doing, and the second asks if the person is at least aware of what else or different might or should be used. In today's climate there are many therapists, sadly perhaps including a number of psychiatrists, who have had but a bare minimum of training in psychotherapy yet who claim to practice it with little or no awareness of their personal limitations. Being limited and *knowing* your limitations may be miles apart.

Persons trained according to any particular theoretical standard are usually of a single mind in reading about or listening to a case and so judge its effectiveness in terms of an implicit collective corpus of knowledge. Persons of different backgrounds naturally hear or find much of a treatment according to what they consider to be the right way of doing things. It is often impossible to distinguish the wrong way of doing things except in terms of what one is trained to believe is correct. Even if one confines one's critique to psychoanalysis and psychotherapy, there are enough distinct schools of treatment to prevent most practitioners from gaining a familiarity with more than a few. A determined Kleinian analyst might well scoff at a self-psychological case report, and this scoffing might rise tenfold if the case was a failure. We will have occasion later to discuss the disparity between psychoanalytic schools that may lead to open hostility and resentment at times. However, we need now merely underscore the fact that the assignment of lack of knowledge as the fundamental cause of a therapeutic failure is hardly a possibility for most appraisals. Indeed, if such a conclusion were reached, it would only occur with like-minded listeners or readers agreeing on obvious deficiencies. Also, it would be well nigh impossible to gather enough representatives from different psychotherapeutic and psychoanalytic schools to agree on anything but the most obvious lack of knowledge. Rather, the culprit, if there be one, is more likely to be singled out as a particular technical mishap.

Although there is no doubt that various psychotherapeutic and psychoanalytic theories agree on a number of concepts such as transference and countertransference, a number of defenses such as denial and repression, and a number of pathological difficulties such as depression and anxiety, it is also true that they diverge on a number of ideas, including the nature of transference and countertransference, the significance of defenses such as denial and repression, and the proper way to consider certain pathologies such as depression and anxiety. Therefore, as we moved away from a lack of knowledge to an investigation of causes of failure stemming from more subtle technical errors, we recognized that this initially would be possible only if all of the appraisals were offered by a group of fairly similarly trained and accordingly indoctrinated therapists.

Self psychology was the theoretical currency employed by the majority of our listeners, and so the mistakes that were made were recognized as reflective of that theoretical perspective. We began with the sine qua non of self psychology, which was making a meaningful empathic connection. That set of words is not much different than establishing a therapeutic alliance or a working alliance, and it is likely that any degree of difference would not be relevant to a study of the cause of a failed case. Some few cases that never seem to get off the ground did seem to qualify for this problem, and so they will be discussed at greater length in Chapter 7.

Self psychology devotes a great deal of effort in unpacking the nuances of empathy, and especially how it echoes, accompanies, or is representative of all manners of countertransference. It is not at all uncommon to connect all failures to countertransference issues, and one does therefore run the risk of reducing all failures to the problems of the analyst or the psychotherapist. Just as our psychopharmacological brothers and sisters prefer to shift blame to the malady or the patient, we must be equally wary of our shifting blame to the problems of the practitioner. There is no doubt that it is an extremely worthwhile exercise to pursue the mistakes of practice, and it is probably true that the bulk of a supervision is directed to that very point. Yet there remains a group of failed cases that do not appear to be a result of a failed analysis of a transference or countertransference issue. We can, of course, revisit a case with that problem in mind, but we should also be free to look elsewhere. Several chapters in this book are devoted to the topics of empathic failure and empathic disruptions (Chapter 13), and sustained empathic immersion (Chapter 14), all elements of the vocabulary of self psychology.

Before tackling the very knotty problem of our capacity to define failure (which we discuss in this chapter) and still struggling with the possible causes of failure, we consider the problem of alternative treatments. This may be no more than a belief or a decision that, as one example, any given patient in psychotherapy might have fared better in psychoanalysis. However, once one's vision is directed away from the very limited training that most of us feel comfortable with, it is necessary to look at the very wide range of alternative therapies. The hard truth is that aside from a few persons who are familiar with and competent enough to perform other therapeutic activities, almost everyone is more or less committed to doing what they do. Some few ego psychologists employ some Kleinian ideas, some few analysts and psychotherapists combine some treatment with medication, some few analysts also employ cognitive-behavioral therapy (CBT) techniques, some few relationalists occasionally think in terms of drives, and on and on with all sorts of qualifications and modifications. For the most part, however, it is not the lack of knowledge or the unfamiliarity with the technique that is the limiting factor in the sharing of ideas and methods. Rather, the insularity of our islands of belief and training has led to a form of national ignorance coupled with hostility that effectively closes off the open exchange of ideas.

For the most part, a patient in psychological distress is unwittingly involved in a therapeutic lottery when seeking treatment. So much depends on one's geographical location (e.g., Jacques Lacan is not popular in the Midwest), one's financial situation (few can afford analytic fees in New York), or one's referring source (physicians refer these days to other physicians for medication), and so on. If the treatment is unsuccessful, then the second chances are often more dismal than the initial lottery because of the limitations and prejudices of the original therapist. The most interesting conclusion that emerged from our very limited study was to be expected and went something like this: "This patient did not do well with the particular treatment and ought to try something else, but we could not say with any sort of sense of assurance just where or what should be considered."

THE DEFINITION

Our final point in the introduction to the concept of failure should have been our initial one, but it was delayed in the hope that some clarity would arrive to help us define just what the definition of failure was. Alas, it just became more difficult to define. The approach to the definition was fourfold. The decision to mark a case as a failure had to come from both therapist and patient, but inasmuch as it was unusual and unlikely to seek out a patient's assessment, we relied on the added judgment of our listening group. These two ratings were then divided into an objective and a subjective group. The first had to do with obvious alterations such as finding a job, getting a divorce, or getting married. The second had to do with the subjective assessment of intangibles such as enjoying life more, no longer contemplating suicide, and the like.

There are many instances of agreement on whether a case is a failure along with a good deal of contention on that supposedly simple but deceptively complex question. It is not unusual to kick off a discussion of this problem with the parallel one of goals. Chapter 12 is devoted to that, but it may be fruitful to begin at that endpoint to further unpack the definition. We can start with an example that may offer a clear instance of a disagreement: cross-dressing. This is a striking demonstration of a goal illustrating divergence. Some patients may wish to rid themselves of this propensity and consider it an unwelcome symptom, some may merely wish to feel less unhappy about the desire, and some may not consider it at all unwelcome. The same series of judgments may exist with the analyst or therapist, but they may not share the same or similar considerations as to the nature of the disorder and its future. If both patient and (say) analyst agree to a goal of erasure of the now "declared" symptom, and if it is successfully eradicated, then failure is not an issue. Inasmuch as this particular concordance of aims is rare, the endpoint may be variations of patient and analyst contentment, ranging all the way from a happy patient coupled with a disappointed analyst to a mutual disappointment. It is difficult to properly place failure in this set of uncertain scenarios. The range is from that of a patient who happily continues to cross-dress joined with an analyst who feels the analysis was a success, to the patient who is unable to feel at all positive about cross-dressing joined with an analyst who feels the analysis came to naught because the symptom remained untouched. Add in an objective observer who insists that the patient was well analyzed, and the problem becomes quite evident as to the proper evaluation of the case. The difference between an external observation and a subjective sense, noted in this chapter, is obvious; adding the two separate perspectives only increases the confusion.

If we revisit the comment about impasses, it can be argued that the problem is not one of a deadlock as much as it is that of ascribing to a normative scale of knowing what is best, and also recognizing what is achievable with the methods at hand.

UNTREATABLE CASES

As a final disposal of the impasse concept, we are confronted with the very difficult problem of the determination of untreatability. The qualifiers that are immediately evident are *by this method or approach* or *by any method or approach*. For many analysts and therapists, the very concept of untreatability is unacceptable, whereas for others it is a not uncommon conclusion, especially if the decision follows from a restricted way of doing things.

Collapsing all failed cases into untreatable cases is the most comfortable way of dealing with failure, because it completely removes the aura of blame and makes it more of a case of bad luck. We shall see (in Chapter 5) how common this is in cases of suicides that succeed. Such unfortunate situations often are reviewed following a variety of heroic measures, and these then allow one to claim that everything was tried and no one can be blamed. One can readily see the dissipation of discomfort that follows from the conclusion of futility. An untreatable case is but an unfortunate and unavoidable failure, and failure is to be accepted. Otherwise, failure may haunt you.

There is no doubt that one way to investigate failed cases in psychoanalysis and psychotherapy would be to collect a large number of so-designated cases and examine a number of variables. One could determine if there were patient gender or age differences, if the length of treatment mattered, if the age or sex of the therapist or analyst was of any consequence, if proponents of one theoretical school had an edge over those of other persuasions, and even if money was a factor. The vagueness and fluidity of the term *failure* would soon cause a halt in the proceedings until some sort of operational definition could be constructed. Perhaps a ranking of dissatisfaction could be formulated in order to accommodate the range of opinions as to what constituted a failure. Sooner or later, the realization would emerge that the analyst or therapist who said, "I have no failures," was not all that different from the one who said, "All of my cases are failures"; in both instances, the nature of failure remains unexamined. Ultimately the new task might take shape, that of determining the essential meaning of failure. That is what this book is about.

The easiest way to solve the vague and uncertain status of failure is to declare it as belonging to a class of *undecidable* and so commit it to the category of personal opinions. Yet it is hard to deny that very often failure is a fact beyond doubt and certainly not only an opinion. That somewhat peculiar standing of fact versus opinion is an invitation to a further analysis. Such an analysis of failure should enable us to better understand what it does to us, how we grapple with what it means to us, and how best to teach others about it. It is, of course, a far cry from what others may hope would be an empirical study.

A word is in order as to why one should *not* consider an empirical study of failed cases, which would gather a large number of cases and thereby attempt to determine some significant parameters and variables peculiar to failed cases. At the very onset of that kind of study, the first stumbling block would be the job of deciding just what would qualify as a failed case and who would make that decision. This is somewhat similar to research measuring the efficacy of various psychotropic medications, but with some striking differences. Drugs for depression and marital therapy for troubled marriages appear at first blush to share a circumscribed problem that demands attention. The difference begins to manifest itself in the somewhat singular nature of depression and the heterogeneous nature of troubled marriages. The unarguably successful treatment or the equally graded failed treatment in each case may be fairly easy to judge, and the same may be said of many other forms of psychological problems. However, most problems do not lend themselves to simple assignment of success or failure; most problems require a subjective assessment of success or failure especially because most problems resist easy labeling and clear remedies. We shall discuss (in Chapter 16) more of the uncertainty regarding the determination of the effectiveness of various treatments, but there are rarely clear-cut answers.

Another problem with a large empirical study is that of knowing what may be significant and what meaningless. Age, sex, money, and geography may not matter a whit, and the number of variables to be considered may add up to a sum with no revelations as to significance.

Forsaking a large-scale empirical study leads to a careful analysis of failure not so much as an endpoint but more as a process with a history and with a variable impact. An analysis of failure should reveal how it unfolds over time, what the possible causes of it may be, how it might be better handled, and especially what it does to us. That is what follows.

3
Facing Failure

When I had the following experience, I felt that other analysts and therapists must have also had similar ones. I soon felt that surely everyone needed to have such an experience, but I could not be certain. It happened after I had been seeing a patient for several years, and after I had become quite familiar with his alternating progress and retreat in treatment. Perhaps I was not quite prepared for his sudden outburst of anger coupled with his suicidal preoccupations. He was ranting at me about how both I and psychoanalysis had failed him, along with his insistence that I give him a pill for his anger and admit to him that this treatment was of no help. As I offered an interpretation as to the meaning behind his rage, I simultaneously and secretly felt that perhaps he was right. Perhaps my belief in the effectiveness of my efforts along with my heartfelt good intentions were just plain wrong. I felt the possible truth of failure along with a somewhat desperate search for alternatives.

As it later turned out, I was probably feeling just as his parents had, at one time, felt about their unhappy son, but at the moment I was totally wrapped in defeat. I was fortunate enough to be able to climb out of my hole of despair, but I was convinced that every physician, psychiatrist, psychotherapist, and psychoanalyst had to know what it was like to feel a failure and to struggle with all the self-doubt and rationalizations that run alongside this sense of defeat. Sometimes we get lucky and manage to either turn such despair into victory or perhaps explain it away. But surely sometimes the patient is right either openly or in some other undeniable way. Perhaps there are those who go through a life of treating others and manage to even sidestep failure, although that is something that I find hard to believe. But above all, I think that such a person has missed out on something very meaningful. We must at some time or another feel that our best efforts are for naught. Because sometimes they really are.

However, the flip side of my quandary soon revealed itself. Another patient, another story, and a whole new set of feelings and wonder. This new narrative was of someone who no one had helped, a patient who was a virtual billboard of failures. Therapist after therapist, drug after drug, and well-thought-out advice after well-thought-out advice had all added up to naught. One could only succeed with such a patient, because surely another failure would be absorbed into this ongoing narrative, whereas a success could only be a triumph. Ambition fueled the hope of success and temporarily blinded the possibility of failures anew.

Success is a sort of aphrodisiac. It is such a positive feeling that it may well insist upon an unrealistic appraisal of an otherwise hopeless situation. We are always situated between these two poles that we call *failure* and *success* but are really carriers of despair or happiness.

Of course, the middle ground is the most rational, reasonable, and obvious. One does the best that one can and proceeds to a number of clichés from "Let the chips fall where they may" to "What will be, will be." Neither the fear of failure nor the glory of success allows one to deviate from the neutrality of just doing one's job. There can be no place for either worries or imaginary applause. Indeed, the neutral position is desirable and necessary, because (says the theory) the extremes tend to tip the therapy. Both eagerness and despair on the therapist's part contaminate the objectivity that must be the therapeutic watchword. Either calls for a form of self-scrutiny that can aid in the conduct of treatment. Whatever the therapist feels should be the product of and demand scrutiny of the treatment itself and not be something that comes from elsewhere. Rather than failure or success with these accompanying emotions preceding the treatment, they must necessarily follow the treatment. There is a danger in expecting too much or too little.

However, such neutrality is only a temporary retreat or a resting place until ambition and/or anxiety returns to the scene. It seems that one or the other must return, because they always seem to participate in one manner or another. Indeed, they regularly drive the treatment and become a necessary companion of it at times. Fear of failure exists in any and every committed therapist, and it alternates with fantasied success. Each allows for variations on the routine and the tried and true alongside a dedication to the tried and true. Somehow we must maintain some equidistance from the extremes of success and failure, but we soon learn that neutrality also has a sense of the unreal within it. Perhaps it might more likely be said to be unstable.

As my patient ranted and raved that I had wasted his time and money, I ran through a number of responses ranging from a drug dosage change to an angry rebuttal of the charges on to regret and remorse. My choice of silence was primarily a result of a lack of options rather than a calculated decision. All of my possible interpretations seemed dated, and no new ones came to mind. My own reluctant embrace of failure appeared to be inevitable, and along with its assured appearance came a litany of excuses that, although they initially arose in a variety of shapes and sizes, fundamentally boiled down to but a single claim to innocence. Somebody else was to blame for this sad state of affairs, and that somebody was probably the patient. Or anyone but me. I later learned that almost everyone who fails as a therapist has a storehouse of excuses that can be called up, examined for usefulness, freely discarded, and just as freely embraced. Failure has no friends. It is ever searching to be shipped elsewhere. When that mode of dissolution is unavailable, then the wish for absolution arrives on the scene. One might expect that something quite different than blame and absolution would appear. In most pursuits from teaching something new to fixing something old, if things go wrong then one looks to doing it differently. We change the time, the sequence, the tools, or the material. Failure serves as an impetus to change. Not so if we are locked into a set way of doing things.

It is difficult to see failure as a friend, but without its regular appearance there can be no hope. Failure drives the engine of improvement, and those who do not know failure or are ever intent on banishing it fail themselves. They cannot go beyond the routine of practice to the arena of innovation. In some peculiar and contradictory manner, we need to look forward to something we do not wish to see. We need to examine and befriend all of the negative aspects of something that is uppermost in our mind to avoid.

MISTAKES AND MISSTEPS

It is important to recognize that it is itself a mistake to think that failure can be reduced to merely doing something wrong. Failure comes in many forms. These forms range from *not* doing something that should have been done to doing something that should *not* have been done on to doing something specifically wrong. And each of these categories has its own set of subcategories that are generally divided quantitatively into too much or too little. To take each in turn very briefly:

1. *Not doing something*: Silence is a common enough phenomenon in psychotherapy and psychoanalysis. Its ubiquity often serves as protection from simply not knowing what to say. One patient reported to me that he could not remember his analyst ever saying anything at all, up to and including the time of this patient announcing that he planned to terminate the treatment. Inasmuch as this analyst did not respond, the patient interpreted the lack of talking as acquiescence and so proceeded to

announce a date for departure. He left without a word from the mute mime and from that point on dismissed and disdained this treatment. Not talking allowed this patient to feel abused and ignored, and we might well imagine that this analyst himself was quite literally at a loss for words.

Interestingly, silence has managed to gain a positive valence that balances its status as a place to hide. Silence allows for the patient to project his or her fantasies onto the analyst, and so it must be endured no matter how much one wishes to speak. It is thus a marvelous rationalization for maintaining muteness as a virtue.

The tug of war between not talking very much and talking too much is, of course, not so much resolved in the determination of the right amount of talking as it is in having something to say. It should be obvious that one can indeed be either verbose or silent as long as what is said or not said is appropriate and relevant and leads to greater understanding. Thus the failure here lies in not talking about what needs to be talked about. That is the mistake.

2. *Doing what should not be done*: This category of therapeutic errors needs to be differentiated from doing something wrong, although excess and error are often collapsed into one. To make this distinction clear, the first consideration of error (i.e., that of doing something that should not be done) is composed of the misapplication or overuse of perfectly acceptable therapeutic technique, whereas the second (i.e., that of doing something wrong) consists of actions that have little or no place in the treatment of a particular patient.

An example of the first is that of a patient who told a story of such a traumatic childhood that it brought tears to the eyes of the listening analyst. This sad tale of woe was one that the analyst was empathic with but was one that led to overidentification and an inability to retain a workable therapeutic distance.

Empathy is regularly included in a list of necessary attributes or, better said, essential aspects of a therapeutic stance. It is considered so critical that the nonempathic analyst or therapist is automatically cast as a failure. As difficult an idea as it may seem to be, one can and should see the inherent danger in its exaggeration and lack of limitation. This particular illustration of excess is to be thought of in contrast to doing something wrong.

3. *Doing something wrong*: What should be the easiest category to define, especially in terms commonly described as *boundary violations*, is often the most difficult to be clear about and the easiest to rationalize. There are a large number of rules to regulate the conduct of most treatments. There are lists of violations and boards of regulators who monitor, evaluate, and mete out punishments for infractions of these rules, and there is no present need to present examples of missteps and misbehavior in carrying out a treatment.

What is perhaps the most egregious form of wrongdoing is not much considered by these organized systems of righting the wrongs, and that is the rather common and oft-committed misdeed of suggesting and offering the wrong kind of treatment.

CASE EXAMPLE

A patient and his wife were constantly arguing with one another and repeatedly threatening one another with divorce. After a psychiatric evaluation, it was suggested that they enter marital therapy, which consisted of being seen together on a weekly basis with an occasional session of one or the other in individual therapy. This particular pursuit of treatment was discontinued after a lengthy period of time and was considered to be unsuccessful by all concerned. Without any appreciable delay, another period of marital therapy with a different therapist was begun and finished with another unsatisfactory result. Over the years the marriage continued in this acrimonious manner, and a series of both individual and couples therapy was entered into. For one period of time the man was placed on antidepressant medication, and the results of this treatment were felt to be equivocal with little change in the marriage but with some diminution in the more emotional and open fighting with one another. After another period of individual therapy, the patient was referred for analytic therapy, which he very reluctantly agreed to try. In rather short order, a marked change in both the patient and the marriage occurred.

This case is not offered to champion one form of therapy over another save to say that the misapplication of treatment can and does occur in many shapes and sizes: Patients in analysis may really need cognitive-behavioral therapy (CBT), patients in CBT may do much better if properly medicated, patients in long-term individual therapy may profit from couples therapy, and so on. We do wrong when we fail to properly prescribe. And we regularly fail to properly prescribe, because we are unfamiliar with alternative approaches out of ignorance, prejudice, greed, or a variety of other excuses or rationalizations. I am sure that this particular form of failure is one most commonly defended by the explanation of meaning well and a lack of clear indications for one form of therapy over another. Good intentions seem to be the hallmark of doing the wrong thing.

Of course, the category of doing the wrong thing applies to all of the discussion in this section, so it must be clear that this final group directs attention primarily to the choice of treatment. The other categories would be subsumed under this last one only after a decision has been made and a course of treatment has begun. Inasmuch as choice is so complex and multifaceted, it is necessary to limit choices to psychotherapy and psychoanalysis and ultimately to individual therapy. Casting too large a web is basically in error inasmuch as few individuals could be expected to make decisions that extend far beyond their personal capabilities.

Within the category of mistaken choice, there are wide differences based on fundamentals, frequency, and even furniture. Some see patients only occasionally, some weekly, some two or three times a week, and some in psychoanalysis four or five times a week, as is necessary. Some give advice, some repair relationships, and some interpret transference to make the unconscious conscious. Some face the patient, and some utilize a couch. Making the choice results from a mix of what is felt is the need of the patient and what is done by the therapist. Often, making a choice allows us to consider failure more openly than usual.

FAILURE AND EXPECTATIONS

One fails as a response to the achievement of one's goals, and here is where vagueness and uncertainty come to the fore. If one has a particular disease with particular symptoms, then removal or eradication of the pathology is the obvious goal. Every treatment involves a normative scale that is eminently clear in certain cases like blood pressure or reactive depression and extremely vague in others such as sexual preferences or happiness. Psychiatry has attempted to dissolve this uncertainty by a combination of delineating careful diagnostic categories in *DSM-IV* (American Psychiatric Association [APA], 2000) and *DSM-V* (APA, forthcoming) and embracing evidence-based treatments for the effectiveness of therapies. But vagueness persists. Patients come for treatment with a variety of issues ranging from sadness to shopping. Some want to get married, and some divorced. Some are sent for treatment, and some are ashamed of wanting treatment. Until and unless a goal is clear and definite and achievable, there can be no failure to correspond to it. And until a therapist accepts a goal as clear and definite and achievable, there can be no struggle to comprehend the reason or reasons for a failure. Unfortunately, the goal of the patient is often not the goal of the therapist, inasmuch as the discrepancy is never made explicit and often never even discussed.

CASE EXAMPLE

Michael called to make an appointment with a psychoanalyst following a meeting called by his business colleagues, who found him extremely difficult to work with. He himself felt he was an easygoing person who did occasionally become impatient with his business associates. The person in the meeting who insisted that Michael see an analyst had herself been in analysis and along with her colleagues had suggested that the possible patient might be depressed; and so together they felt they had eased the path for a psychological evaluation. This putative patient did not feel at all depressed but was quite willing and even eager to be examined. He balked at the idea of himself undergoing psychoanalysis, and indeed after one or two sessions felt no need to undergo treatment of any sort. He was clearly not yet a patient. The analyst offered several options to be considered by this possible patient. These ranged from psychoanalysis to psychotherapy to an occasional meeting, but the goals of both Michael and the analyst were really unable to be clearly articulated. However, there is no doubt of a striking disparity between the two if a goal could be made explicit. The analyst might say something about insight making this man a more congenial person (i.e., effecting a character change). The nonpatient might hope that his colleagues would see him as more cooperative. There was no meeting of the minds.

A few months later, another appointment was made and a bona fide patient seemed to emerge. The business was not doing well, and his associates were beginning to want someone to blame. All of the criticisms that he originally seemed not to hear became audible to him. This possibly new patient struggled with his own conflict over blaming business conditions or himself. He tried to minimize his faults. All he had to do was be more patient and listen better. Perhaps he had to become a different person, in which case he himself would have to own the problem and so begin to share a common goal with the analyst. The goal of the patient, however, was not quite consonant with that of the analyst inasmuch as the latter's concept of analyzability required a great deal more than mere discontent and unhappiness. Michael seemed interested in being a patient of some sort, but he was far from a suitable candidate for analysis.

Altering what may have been an unrealistic goal, the analyst wondered if Michael were treatable. That new category would be broad enough and wide enough to entail an entirely different consideration of goals. Sooner or later, the goal needed to move from a locus outside of the patient to one that resided in himself. Only when the patient assumed ownership of some form of pathology could an alteration be contemplated.

Many treatments go awry because of a failure in agreed-upon goals, but this particular form of failure ranges from properly locating the goal to always shifting the status of the goal. Goals are altered and modified during the course of treatment, and often these changes are not made explicit. If a patient who professed a determination to get married decided over time that perhaps he or she would be better off remaining single, would that be attributed to a negotiated compromise or to a bad decision inasmuch as marriage may be felt to be a sign of health? Can one alter a goal without deviating from a normative scale?

COMPROMISES

Sigmund Freud (1925) spoke of curability of symptoms by describing how they could be resolved by psychoanalysis. This meant that the unearthing of the unconscious would essentially eliminate the core component of the symptom. Patients come for treatment of symptoms that occur after a particular external event such as a loss or other trauma, after having a symptom occur without any particular initiating factor, or simply to alleviate a lifelong characterological condition. If psychoanalysis is suggested, it is assumed that the removal of whatever unconscious factors are operating may well lead to the removal of symptoms in any of these three categories. However, symptom removal for some takes a secondary position to insight into the unconscious, and Maxwell Gitelson insisted that the removal of symptoms was but a byproduct of the understanding achieved by psychoanalysis (Goldberg, 2001). People are advised to have analysis primarily to better understand themselves, and in that pursuit they may well feel better. We shall pursue this point in Chapter 12.

Of course, there is something unreal about relegating feeling better to a state of uncertainty akin to happenstance. It does, however, enable one to advise everyone who *can* be analyzed to *be* analyzed without concern about any personal improvement above and beyond such personal insight. Thus, persons with the acute onset of a symptom after an external event may well improve with a variety of procedures, including psychoanalysis. Persons with an inexplicable onset of a symptom are perhaps more likely to be considered for psychoanalysis, whereas those with long-standing characterological difficulties are often sent to be analyzed as something like a court of last resort. Here is where we often compromise on our goals, and so here is where failure becomes an elusive concept.

It is often true that the pursuit of psychodynamic psychotherapy is less of a disappointment than that of psychoanalysis. The latter, despite the Gitelson caution, regularly promises more and regularly disappoints. Therapy manages to fulfill a goal that is limited and clear. Analysis is so open-ended and unlimited in its efforts that it is often doomed to falling short. Thus, one requirement of an analysis is ratcheting down one's ambitions even if that does not present itself in the transference.

At times, however, it is an important factor in the transference with a reappearance of a parental imago who expects so much of a child as well as of himself or herself. The failure that frightened me in my angry patient revealed itself to be the carrier of a dual message (i.e., the analyst who did not cure and the parent who did not properly parent). At one time, my patient's father asked him (the patient) if he (the father) had been a good father. The need for such reassurance could occur only against the background of a hidden reproach that was never completely unspoken. My patient was trapped in his answer, because he could neither forgive nor forget, and his rage at this entrapment expressed itself in his tirade against me. The truth of the parental failure along with that of the analytic failure is never unadorned. Perhaps every analysis is less than it should be.

SUCCESS

Some time ago I attended a conference, one part of which was for the different schools or theories of psychoanalysis to present their ideas in a sort of competition of recognition. As one representative of one school began to present a case for demonstration, a colleague turned to whisper to me that this particular presenter regularly and repeatedly presented this particular case on a number of occasions despite it being several years old. My whisperer's point was that this was the only successful case of this presenter's career, and so he trotted it out on any and all occasions. This memory serves to highlight the sad state of affairs about success.

Success has a slippery status. As noted in the reference to goals in this chapter, there is an uncertain consensus as to what constitutes a success. If a patient initiates a treatment with a clear endpoint in mind, and this goal is one with which the therapist agrees, then success is unequivocal if attained. I have no idea as to the overall achievement of such mutual states of agreement, but I suspect that they are rare and are made so by the ongoing process. Once an analysis or psychotherapy is begun, there is an inherent modification of the aims of the treatment.

CASE EXAMPLE

Earlier, the case of a cross-dressing man who entered psychoanalysis with the avowed hope of ending his wish to dress as a woman was presented. His analyst agreed with the goal and proceeded with an analysis that, to all intents and purposes, seemed to be a success, save for the fact that the patient continued to cross-dress. The patient was quite pleased with the analysis and later wrote to the analyst confirming this feeling as well as indicating that the success was a lasting one. This particular evaluation of the patient resulted from his feeling good in many areas of his life up to and including his cross-dressing. The analyst felt otherwise. How could the persistence of cross-dressing be anything but a failure? The process may have gone well, but the end result was a dismal one.

This case serves not only to represent the disparate views of the two participants in the treatment, but also to underscore the uncertainty about the very idea of what is to be considered pathological and deviant versus what is a matter of choice.

For the most part, every physician, psychiatrist, psychotherapist, and psychoanalyst tries to do his or her best and begins every treatment with the hope of success. One may fear failure, but one never anticipates it. Although we may keep some sense of failure in mind, we never contemplate embracing it, but we always are intent on banishing it. It therefore should not be a surprise that our focus on success routinely tends to blind us to failure. We are unable to really look failure in the face, and thus it is only scrutinized as a lack of success. Yet it is possible that failure merits an examination in its own right (i.e., not as a lack but as a tangible and comprehensible entity). As noted in this chapter, failure has multiple forms that range from not doing something to doing the wrong thing. However, behind all of these forms there exists a network of causes and reasons. It is often the case that we look to why we did wrong or did not do right only if we are forced to do so.

It may sound quite perverse, but it may profit us to pause at those crossroads of choice. Such choices range from agreeing to see and treat certain patients to advising one sort of treatment over another to doing one process of a specific treatment over another and on and on. Failure exists at all of these points of decision. We may choose without full knowledge of the alternatives, or we may choose because of a personal need to pursue one road over another or because of poor advice. Whatever we choose often stills the other possibility, and this pause may be necessary for us to pursue our decision with vigor and resolve. At times this chosen path fails to gain total commitment, and one or more alternatives haunt the treatment throughout. Say a patient is seen in weekly therapy, and one continues to entertain and even worry about more or less frequent meetings. It is even possible that such a continual sense of doubt may help the process, because it remains possible that keeping failure alive is not necessarily a detriment.

All failure is a mutual construction, and the contributors to this joint endeavor are the aspirations of the therapist or analyst and the expectations of the patient. The disappointment that characterizes the feeling of failure is not always equally shared and so is a result of a negotiation. The blame that accompanies this negative emotion of disappointment is also one of mutual construction, but this is rarely equally shared. Psychoanalysts know that this sequence of hope followed by disappointment and succeeded by blame is a familiar one of childhood, one fueled by ambition and grandiose fantasies. We struggle to separate the irrational components behind our hope and despair from the realistic factors that might properly evaluate and ultimately standardize success and failure. Unfortunately, only the extremes of success and failure are easily rated. Objectivity is lost as our personal subjective interests participate in the negotiating process. Therefore, failure, like many concepts, may well be something that we cannot precisely define, but we know when we see it. That is, if we choose to look.

4

Dismissing Failure

The investigation of failed cases in psychoanalysis and dynamic psychotherapy proved to be more difficult than one might imagine, and, in retrospect, it was naïve to think otherwise. This realization began when an initial effort was made to recruit analysts and therapists to present their failed cases to a seminar. The very common initial reaction of many was to laugh, say they had no failures, and quickly walk away. One person said that he simply had no time and was briefly stunned to hear that it required only a little over one hour; he quickly recovered when he learned of the day of the week for our meetings, insisted that that day was impossible, and then quickly walked away. Several persons appeared to be visibly shocked and insulted, and they seemed to be at a loss for words. A good number of respondents insisted either that they kept no notes or that their notes were lost, with one very cooperative person sadly reporting that all his particular notes of one case were lost in a fire. One person agreed to present, but the following day he yelled across a long hall that he could not and quickly walked away. Some few said that they simply could not do it and could not go much beyond that. At least one agreed to present a failed case but ended up presenting a successful one, which, he said, at one point seemed to be a failure until he turned it around.

The initial innocence of this inquiry changed to a curiosity as to just why so many therapists were too frightened to expose and subject their failed cases to a postmortem analysis. It might seem to be quite evident that any failure from a medical mishap to an automotive accident asks for a careful study in order to avoid recurrences. However, we do know, or soon find out, that when automobiles are recalled or when hospitals review unfortunate endpoints with patients, there is an immediate reaction of denial or dismissal. Automotive manufacturers do it to protect their sales. Hospitals do it to protect their image. When the solution to a mishap is found, the reactions are varied but ultimately culminate in relief and assurance that the error will not happen again. It does seem different with our field. Hospitals and automobile makers are able to be impersonal institutions, although at times one or more persons may take the fall. However, analysts and psychotherapists all take failure personally. On a few occasions, a student candidate would present a case with a clear indication that he or she had done what their supervisor had insisted be done, and if it came to grief it was surely not their fault. Of course, that is close to "The dog ate my homework" and is a clear message aimed at avoiding blame. This cardinal issue of blame became apparent when we began to interview the presenters and their reaction to the experience of exposing their failures.

THE PRESENTATION OF A FAILED CASE

By no means are we able to go much beyond some general reactions to our case presentations and to offer some ideas about what exposing one's work means to those who were willing to do so. Perhaps a large-scale study could be more definitive about the vicissitudes of presenting one's case to an audience of therapists, but one major variable is the composition of the listeners and one's familiarity with those who are in a position to judge and evaluate what is a very personal experience.

Almost all of the presenters, when asked why they decided to present, gave reasons that one would readily characterize as positive, ranging from wishing to learn more to wanting to share an interesting experience. Again, a large number of them reported about the experience by claiming it to be anything but a positive experience. The complaints ranged from describing it as a "sadomasochistic" exercise of the group to feeling that the listeners became unruly and overstimulated. Yet there was a near unanimous impression that it was a worthwhile undertaking, and one they would do again. It sounded for some much like going to the dentist, and for others like attending church. The positive remarks had to do with looking at the case in a different light, recognizing mistakes, and gaining a better feel for the patient's state of mind. There was thus an intermingling of the negative and the positive to underscore the impression of a painful yet necessary ordeal. It would appear that the presenters differed from the avoiders in some meaningful psychological sense, from being less sensitive to criticism to being surer of themselves. Everyone, however, seemed to care.

One presenter likened his experience to that of a minor traumatic state with an anxiety dream that followed. The psychic reorganization that follows such a traumatic event can be productive in the sense of learning more, or at times destructive as one may continue to feel the disruption that manifests itself in a longer lasting anxiety and anger. Perhaps that is why so many potential presenters had to avoid the risk of such a possible disruption, and also why there was such an intense concentration on the responsiveness of the audience. This may also explain why there was an almost unanimous decision to do it again if asked. In fact, without being asked, a few offered to present again if there were openings.

The questions that arise in our effort to understand failure are undoubtedly connected to the presenting therapist or analyst who serves as judge or referee in the determination of an individual failure. That directs our attention to the reasons that these presenters offered for the failure and especially how they coincide with or differ from those offered by the listeners. Surely those who avoided presenting took the task as representative of a personal failure, whereas those eager to present may have felt less personally responsible for the failure.

THE CAUSES

As noted in Chapter 2, when asked about the cause of the case failure, very few attributed the problem to a lack of knowledge on the part of the therapist. Rather the fault, if there was one, lay in the area of the therapeutic relationship with such issues as a countertransference problem, an empathic failure, or whatever was felt to conform to that particular critic's way of thinking and formulating cases. As long as one remained within the agreed-upon arena of theoretical thinking, then failure would result from improper function or performance rather than from not knowing. With a preponderance of self psychologists in attendance, the focus became the nature of the empathic connection, but in all likelihood others may have felt the major issue could have been the nature of the interpretation of the compromise formation or a host of other possibilities. Not knowing what to do was reduced to an inability to notice and comprehend the problem and so was differentiated from an ignorance of what would have been the proper way to behave. Thus, to claim that the presentation allowed the therapist to have "a better sense of the patient's state of mind" makes the point of a deficiency in understanding more fully, and clearly this was different from that of not recognizing the need to better "sense the patient's state of mind."

In presenting a failed case to a group of like-minded analysts and therapists, one is engaging in something akin to a group supervision. There is a shared background of beliefs, and one can imagine how discordant it might be if someone steeped in Kleinian or Lacanian ideas would present to an ego psychologist. If one were to deviate too far from the acceptable vocabulary and set of ideas, then the entire concept of failure would need to be reconsidered. Staying safely within the community of those who speak the same language and share a common history allows for a tacit agreement on the normative scale that one employs to gauge proper treatment as well as success and failure.

PLACING THE BLAME

An article in a psychiatric journal (Brent et al., 2009), which we will expound upon in Chapter 5, portrayed "treatment resistance" in depressed adolescents and assumed that the therapist or psychiatrist was in no way responsible for treatment failures that, according to this peculiar play of words, were due to the disease that resided in the patient, and so it or the patient was resisting the treatment. The article made no mention of psychotherapy outside of cognitive-behavioral therapy (CBT) and so would naturally enlist a different group of concerned treaters. The sense of failure is only that of either CBT or the medication, and the measure of success or failure is a judgment of either the therapist in terms of symptoms or the patient in terms of well-being. The latter may allow a commonality with psychotherapy, but it calls into question the entire process of deciding what works.

If we restrict our inquiry to psychoanalysis and psychotherapy, we are surely as guilty as are our medicating friends in not becoming familiar enough with what others do and what they may be able to achieve. The walls that have been built are impervious to the transmission of knowledge. I suspect there are instances in almost any analyst's or psychotherapist's practice that involve a patient who is receiving a medication while in analysis or therapy. Often these dual forms of treatment are conducted by dual practitioners, and often the two rarely if ever communicate with one another. The therapist involved in a psychological activity may or may not keep abreast of the different modes of action of psychotropic drugs, let alone the varied dosages. All sorts of explanations and rationalizations are offered to explain what would ordinarily be considered either unacceptable or at least unwise. Just as analysts know that patients develop transference reactions to both medications and medicators, so, too, do psychopharmacologists know of the power of placebo effects offered by both medication and psychologic interpretation.

There are a number of solutions to the problem of these particular different forms of dual treatment for one patient. One answer is to maintain a strict separation, which primarily consists of an absence of sharing of information. Another is to have a good deal of contact and communication but with a clear division of power and expertise. A third is to have both activities residing in but one person who is able both to prescribe and to conduct therapy or analysis. Much of the decision as to which of the solutions to pursue depends, of course, on the qualifications and competence of the person or persons conducting the treatment. It does seem at least possible that some cases fail because the particular needs of the patient as to the ideal use, nonuse, or occasional use of medication are not evaluated for how to best accomplish this. Unfortunately, the decision is made based upon practical reasons that override the differences between patients. If one cannot write prescriptions or is unfamiliar with the varieties of transference, the issue of what is best for a particular patient is put to the side. One rarely hears of referring a patient who may require both dynamic psychotherapy and psychotropic medications with the primary consideration being what combination of providers would best serve the patient. Practicality rules the day.

THE PROBLEM OF PARADIGMS

Within psychoanalysis and psychotherapy, another striking division of labor has arisen. I recently ran across two blatant examples in reading a book and an article, each written by eminent psychoanalysts. The book (Ellman, 2010) is a review of major contributors to psychoanalytic theory and is composed of outstanding reviews of the familiar great names from Sigmund Freud to Melanie Klein to Wilfred Bion and beyond. Alas, there is no consideration of Jacques Lacan. The author claims that he was too unfamiliar with Lacan to include him. The article, on the other hand, is directed against almost all of psychoanalytic thinking outside of Lacan (Fink, 2010). The article references only Lacan's work, save for one reference in French and one to Thomas Kuhn. The article is a diatribe against the central position of "understanding" in psychoanalysis, but proceeds without a clear comprehension of what that word means to anyone other than the author. The book is aimed at a careful exposition of psychoanalytic theorists and how they share some ideas and differ in others. It is more in the direction of integration.

Surely Lacan is a significant enough figure in analytic thinking and theorizing who deserves consideration. But just as surely is the obvious fact that the concept of *Verstehen* or understanding is a contentious issue. Like the psychopharmacologist who had no place in his therapeutic armamentarium for dynamic psychotherapy, many analysts and psychotherapists are equally locked into their way of thinking.

ALTERNATIVE TREATMENTS

The relevance of our isolated islands of practice and knowledge was brought home to us by the very large number of members of our seminar who suggested that failed cases are not to be considered untreatable without their being treated with "alternative treatments." Unfortunately, there were no specific directions given as to how to choose amongst alternative treatments, primarily because no one knew much about them. Just as the psychopharmacologist is able to dismiss the embrace of failure by the appellation of "treatment resistance" and fail to consider psychotherapy, so too is the analyst or psychotherapist able to sidestep and likewise dismiss the uncomfortable feeling of failure by suggesting that some other form of treatment might do the trick. The highest probability is that neither knows much about the other. And the "other" for psychoanalysis and psychotherapy extends to anyone who differs from ourselves.

Just as it is true that not everyone who can be analyzed should be analyzed and not everyone can be analyzed, it is also true that we are presently not able to differentiate those who can from those who cannot as well as those who should from those who should not. Is it also possible that not everyone who can undergo a Lacanian analysis or a self-psychological one also fulfills the above conundrum about choice and selection? To complicate matters even further, are we at all capable of distinguishing who might benefit from the one rather than the other? Is it not rather commonplace to make the assumption that if one theoretical approach falls to ruin, then that particular mode of treatment is not just feasible (i.e., the analysis was a failure, so the patient is unanalyzable)? Does an ego psychologist refer an analytic patient to a Kleinian or a Bionian because he or she knows full well that this "alternative" approach is really warranted? Aside from the unlikelihood of this ever happening, are not other factors responsible? The psychopharmacologist may refer a patient for analysis after other efforts have been exhausted but rarely before that point. The qualifications that seem to need to be attached to the tag of *untreatability* are (a) by this particular person using (b) this particular form of treatment at (c) this particular time after (d) considering conjunctive treatment and (e) with full awareness of the applicability of other modes of treatment.

The comfort that ensues from belonging to one group of persons who see things alike and often are dismissive of other approaches is periodically buttressed by claiming that the others are simply wrong or that one has neither time nor energy to change a much-used and valuable perspective. Brenner (1955) some time ago made the observation that became a hallmark of many psychoanalysts: that everything psychological can and should be seen as a compromise formation. Aside from the emptiness of that declaration inasmuch as it fails to allow any one notion to be differentiated from another (they are both compromise formations as is just about everything), it opens the door to an action that radically undermines our ability to meaningfully communicate with one another.

ALL THEORIES WORK

Some time ago, after I became familiar with psychoanalytic self psychology, I also learned that I could see everything as some sort of a narcissistic disorder. This capacity allows one to rather easily dismiss other ways of investigation. However, I soon realized that just about everyone is able to restrict his or her vision to one set of theoretical lenses. Object relations theory is an equally powerful theoretical tool under which to subsume all data. The same can be said of Kleinian theory or of Bionian, Lacanian, or interpersonal theory. The marvelous appeal of a Brenner type of statement fails to allow—or, better said, forces one to an inevitable conclusion as to what is the best way to see things. Like it or not, only failure forces us to look elsewhere.

When one learns or ascribes to a particular way of doing things or looking at things, it becomes routine to defend that way whether it be a theory or a way of life. Thomas Kuhn (1970) has best described the failure of dialogue when he wrote that when

> two scientific schools disagree about what is a problem and what a solution, they will inevitably talk through each other when debating the merits of their respective paradigms. In the partially circular argument that regularly results, each paradigm will be shown to satisfy more or less the criteria that it dictates for itself and to fall short of those dictated by its opponents. (pp. 109–110)

Stepansky (2009) has beautifully demonstrated how attempts at integration all fall short. No one, however, has dared to suggest that reconciliation and dialogue are futile. Perhaps we need to recognize the present state of affairs in a more positive way. We really cannot do more than agree to disagree while we remain fixed in our disagreements. As long as your method is effective, you become wedded to it and may even try to convince others of its worth. True believers are often proselytizers. The initial reaction to the failure of your method is to examine whether it was applied correctly, and so how to remedy your error. It is a performance problem. However, it often takes a number of such failures before one looks elsewhere. Stepansky (2009) told us that usually these groups of varied theories resemble separate and often competitive fiefdoms with separate journals and separate institutes of training. An inner orthodoxy develops, and so people are characterized as not being "real analysts" or "real Kleinians" in a negative judgment, or sometimes are labeled as "classical self psychologists" in perhaps a more positive light. Allegiances and membership not only breed group solidarity but also often encourage contempt and dissent toward other groups. Heroes and heroines within the groups become idealized and can become sources of inspiration as well as founders of new groups and subgroups. It often takes a rather severe disappointment or disillusionment to turn one's back on a group to which you have both allegiance and a number of other benefits. These moments of disaffection are often based upon personality differences rather than intellectual ones.

Failure sits unhappily in this collection of disparate theories and allegiances. It is almost required to be dismissed as but a mistake in application rather than a fundamental error of the method. In truth, it is not an error of the theory or method so much as it is a shortcoming. If we ascribe to the possibility or probability that every theory can be utilized to explain and understand any patient, we are required and expected to compare them as to which is preferable to whom and when. Rather than integrate the divergent theories, as some do (Ellman, 2010), or to insist that one is wrong and one is right (Mitchell, 1988), one might move to a position that some work well for one patient and one analyst or therapist and some for others. The question, then, becomes which approach is best under a certain particular set of conditions, and thus an incidence of failure becomes a relative thing (i.e., relative to both analyst or therapist and patient).

If we are able to effect a mind-set that relinquishes the notion of a singular approach to clinical material, we soon find that our ideas about success also require rethinking. Just as we try mightily to dismiss failure, we yearn to embrace success. The fact of the matter is that some patients will improve by working with a number of different therapists utilizing a variety of approaches. It may be the case that we are luckier in succeeding and unlucky in failing. That is a hard pill for many to swallow, but our history shows that loads of people have been helped before any of our heroes and heroines arrived. This is certainly not to say that others were not helped, nor is it meant to denigrate any of the contributions made by our many teachers. It is merely to insist that the problem of application remains.

RECAPITULATION

Both success and failure deserve and demand a careful psycho-analytic investigation just as the sense of pride and the sense of defeat each requires a dispassionate study. Unfortunately, we welcome one and dismiss the other. No doubt, different theoretical approaches will employ a different lexicon, and that I choose one rather than another merely illustrates an earlier point.

Success can best be equated with a rise in one's self-esteem and so may be explained by an allowable expression of a grandiose fantasy. A wish to be acknowledged and recognized may be fueled by the fantasy of fame and is often associated with dreams of flying and occasionally with a fear of overstimulation. In line with this way of theoretical thought, failure is a drop in self-esteem with a concomitant fear of hollowness and depression. Each of these possible extremes of self-esteem can be called upon to regulate the other.

Beyond a thumbnail sketch of these affect states related to one's handling of a case, we also may at times see a particular form of transference related to the case.

CASE EXAMPLE

The earlier noted case in which I felt the painful and disabling feeling of failure is also illustrative of the patient's transference of his own father's struggle with failure. This patient was able to express his intense rage and disappointment at his father's rather sporadic and futile efforts to be a proper parent. This man would insist on taking his son on a boat ride but would soon demonstrate his ineptness at sailing or managing the boat. He was always at a loss as to how to comfort his son, so he could only announce that "the crying must stop." However, in later life he would regularly plead with his son to tell him that he was a good father.

As I became wrapped in failure, I seemed mainly determined to not be the incarnation of that sad man, inasmuch as I felt, in my mind, the wish for the analysis to be successful. No doubt this is a familiar enough cognitive conflict in many treatments, but there may be a prolonged delay in one being able to separate the struggle of the transference from the reality of the moment. It becomes a counterintuitive battle to feel good about feeling bad long enough to make sense of the latter. However, only by feeling good about feeling bad could I emancipate myself from the latter, but paradoxically that highlighted what I wished to be rid of. An easier way out was to fall into despair just enough to assign it elsewhere. As will be clear in Chapter 15, only the persistence of the feeling of failure allowed me to solve the problem.

THE REWARDS OF FAILING

The urge to rid oneself from the feeling of failure no doubt enlists a number of efforts to be effective. To dismiss failure rather than embrace it seems obvious, yet only by the latter can we hope to understand it. In fact, failure offers an opportunity, because it is the primary impetus to try something different, to look elsewhere and to encourage creativity.

Asking a psychoanalyst or a psychotherapist to present a failed case is often felt as an invitation to reexperience an anxiety associated with a loss of self-esteem. Only if it can be investigated in a dispassionate way, or by an uninvolved third party, is there hope for a benefit to the inquiry. One is then able to properly consider it and classify it to determine if it is unavoidable or capable of further understanding. Surely if we do everything right and make no mistakes, our treatments should succeed. If not, something went wrong either from our doing the wrong thing or due to the fault of the patient. It turns out that each of these possibilities is a lot more complicated than it first may seem.

5

Deconstructing Failure

We have said that failure has no friends. It sits obdurate and unhappily between dismissal and denial, but it is never seen on anyone's dance card. Rather, it is shunned and often forgotten. Some time ago, when I was a candidate at an analytic institute, one of my star teachers bragged (although he did say it in a matter-of-fact manner) that all of the cases that he had supervised had stayed in analysis until they were finished. Thus he had an enviable and unblemished record of success. Now the implications of that position are enormous, because it is not at all unusual for analytic candidates to lose cases, and indeed one of the major achievements of one's analytic training is to keep a case, any case, until the requisite number of hours is attained, and/or especially to have an analytic case terminate the analysis successfully. One could only admire and hope to emulate this outstanding bit of good fortune. Either this rather unusual person had managed to select only those cases that seemed likely to finish; or else he was so adept at the management of his students who were in supervision with him that he handled all of the untoward countertransference reactions that were seemingly inevitable; or, in the most unlikely scenario to me at that time, he had a wholly different conceptualization of the ending of treatment. Above all, the wholly alien idea that he had had the misfortune to miss out on something that could be of value never seemed to occur to him.

The message that was implicit in my teacher's announcement was a clear one. Success was available to everyone who chose wisely, and who made no mistakes, and so failure was never to be seen as inevitable. In fact, it seemed to be totally avoidable. Of course, that means that one never gets to carefully investigate or study failure per se, which becomes defined only as a lack of success rather than as something that has its own characteristics and content. All of disease, for example, is clearly seen and regularly defined as the negative of health, but disease also makes a claim to be studied in its own right. Pathology of all sorts is considered to be a subject of great interest and complexity that is investigated with the implicit assumption of its relationship to health but with no acknowledgment of this assumption. In psychoanalysis and psychotherapy, we study the particular failures in growth and development that may result in psychopathology. We also study the content of neuroses and psychoses, again with the unspoken conviction that our ultimate goal is their eradication, yet with a spirit of inquiry that allows an objectivity that is essential for learning. Not so for the pathology of treatment, which is treated with disdain, contempt, and occasionally sympathy. The fact that one takes treatment failures personally and disease impersonally would suggest that objectivity is even more crucial to the investigation of treatment failures.

The crucial factor in the deployment and investigation of failure appears to be the personal one—is it the fault of the analyst or therapist that brought the case to ruin, or does the fault lie outside? One solution has been devised by general psychiatry, a solution that effectively sidesteps any personal involvement and allows only a touch of responsibility. It is a prime example of how personal feelings inhibit a proper scientific study of treatment failure.

ON THE VERY IDEA OF "TREATMENT RESISTANCE"

As noted in Chapter 4, a recent issue of the *American Journal of Psychiatry* featured an article on suicide in adolescence that underlined and delineated a group that was considered resistant to treatment (Brent et al., 2009). That group bore the acronym of TORDIA (treatment of resistant depression in adolescence) and had a history of a variety of unsuccessful therapeutic interventions. Not surprisingly, there was no mention of psychoanalytically oriented or psychodynamic treatment as one of the interventions. Most readers would or perhaps might conclude that the multiple authors of this article either dismissed psychodynamic psychotherapy and/or had had no training in it. Cognitive-behavioral therapy (CBT) was listed as the psychological treatment that was offered—again unsuccessfully. The particular reference to this article is not meant as a criticism of it, because the authors probably had only a limited familiarity with psychoanalytic thinking. Rather, it is representative of a feeling of defeat or resignation on the part of the psychiatrists who focus on factors involved in predicting suicide rather than in ameliorating it. I take this feeling of despair as a possible clue to understanding some cases of suicide, and I should like to expand that concept, one that might more properly be considered a form of countertransference, to see if it can be of assistance in the treatment of some suicidal patients. This is not to be seen as only critical of the above-mentioned article; it reflects a common lack of consideration of the ways in which a therapist's feelings should become a proper ingredient in doing or choosing treatment.

CASE EXAMPLE

A young man was presented to a psychiatric conference as a case of intractable depression. He had been treated with a variety of antidepressant medications, cognitive-behavioral therapy, and electric shock treatments. He was a pleasant and affable person who was ever preoccupied with committing suicide, much to the consternation and concern of the psychiatrist, who was at his wit's end as to what to do about or for his patient. This treating psychiatrist felt that it was very difficult for him to relate to the patient, and he feared that the patient would ultimately succeed in killing himself. The patient was hospitalized and given another course of electroconvulsive therapy (ECT), which seemed to eliminate the suicidal ideation but only for a short time. The psychiatrist sought supervision inasmuch as he felt totally at a loss as to what more he could do for this patient. The supervisor asked if this patient had ever had intensive psychotherapy or analysis or had even been considered for it. The answer was in the negative both because this psychiatrist was not an analyst and because he did not feel the patient could afford analysis. The suggestion was given that the patient be referred to a clinic, but before this could be done the patient successfully suicided. When the psychiatrist returned to report this sad news to the aforementioned supervisor, he discussed both his own remorse at the futility of his efforts along with the general feeling amongst the hospital personnel, who knew of and remembered this patient, that this suicide was inevitable and nothing more could have been done.

Once again, feelings of defeat and hopelessness seemed to dominate the situation with all of the involved personnel sharing a conviction that "treatment resistance" meant exactly that—they were all at their wit's end, and nothing more could have been done. When the parents of this deceased young man went to see the psychiatrist, they openly struggled with the possibility that perhaps they had failed in some way and wondered how culpable they were. The psychiatrist quickly and firmly assured them that no one was to blame, that everything had been tried, and that their guilt was irrational.

Of course, it would be foolhardy to suggest that this stance of the psychiatrist was in error and equally foolhardy to entertain the thought that intensive psychotherapy or analysis might have done the trick. Rather, this case is presented as an illustration of the emotional experience that characterized this case along with the ones noted in the Brent et al. (2009) article. The experience is that of helplessness, and the inquiry suggested is one that encourages a better understanding of that emotion. Outside of having a personal analysis and/or conducting a therapeutic analysis of the patient that would allow such a more detailed comprehension of the state of mind, it is unlikely that anyone would end up anywhere but at an impasse.

At the present state of our knowledge about suicide and depression, there seems to be no clear guideline as to what treatment works best for what patient. Both the multiplicity of available therapies alongside the variety of convinced opinions make for a possible game of chance for any particular patient. The psychiatrist or therapist who insists on medication alone or on psychotherapy alone is taking an unwarranted risk in the decision process. The psychiatrist or therapist who is unfamiliar with or untrained in psychopharmacology or psychotherapy is likewise taking a risk in the treatment process. The training program that is unable or unwilling to offer a variety of skills training for students or residents is best seen as limited to partial training. The only way to determine the best treatment for any patient is to operate from a position without prejudice and predetermined certainty.

Cases of potential suicide try our therapeutic zeal. The pressure to declare any patient or group of patients as treatment resistant is an opportunity to examine the reasons for such a declaration and so to inquire as to whether that decision may be a clue to the origins of the patient's psychopathology. Psychiatrists and psychodynamic therapists are or should be uniquely able to determine if their own emotional state is reflective of a particular transference–countertransference configuration. Such an opportunity is often waylaid by a predetermined prejudice as to what constitutes effective treatment and what allows the labeling of someone as treatment resistant. The psychiatrists involved in this case managed to stand outside of the treatment and considered their personal reactions, in this case of despair and helplessness, not to matter as far as the fate of the man was concerned. They concluded their non-involvement by a declaration of hopelessness. I believe this feeling, one that is free of fault finding, becomes the major impediment to a scientific investigation of failure.

UNTREATABLE

The feelings of hopelessness and despair that characterized the situation following the suicide of the patient in the "On the Very Idea of 'Treatment Resistance'" section of this chapter differ a great deal from those for patients for whom no hope was ever entertained. The rescue fantasies that accompany the efforts to treat difficult or "treatment-resistant" patients was probably not at all much activated in a patient considered to be untreatable from the start, no matter how rarely that appellation is used. There often are no clear-cut parameters to employ in the decision to classify a patient as untreatable, because the evaluation so depends upon the person doing the evaluating. One man's ambition may be another man's folly, and so this particular tag may be inextricably linked to the activation of rescue fantasies, which in turn often can lead to the ensuing sense of failure.

No matter what particular form of treatment is being considered, there are particular rescue fantasies regularly associated with it. In one discussion of analyzability, a distinction was made that made clear that one must preface the prospects of treatability with the clause "utilizing this form of treatment." Thus, this is an admonition that one must exhaust all forms of treatment before making a decision. As long as one does not stimulate hope and the fantasy of rescue is dormant, then despair is kept at arm's length. There is no doubt that the wish to avoid the discomfort of despair robs us of our objectivity.

No greater hidden pleasure exists than the effective treatment of someone who frustrated or defied the efforts of another therapist. Of course, this applies to action both within and between forms of therapy from analyzing someone successfully who had not been so analyzed by someone else, to medicating someone with a combination of meds not utilized before, on to successfully employing psychotherapy to a CBT failure, and so on. There seems to be no element that is intrinsic to the quality of untreatability. However, surely there are patients who everyone would agree are beyond rescue. They are so uncooperative or so fixed in their illness or unable to fit in any form of therapy that there would be a universal agreement on their untreatability. However, times change, and so do our certainties.

For many years, male and female homosexuality was included on a list of pathology, despite many cries for their removal. Certain groups of therapists (Socarides, 1995) made claim to success in curing what were considered to be sexual perversions. As more data were accumulated, these forms of behavior became depathologized or delisted from the ranks of the diseased. In a brief period of time, the failure to cure a homosexual was transformed from a failed treatment to what may have been a success in those cases in which the patient became comfortable with his or her sexual orientation, and the supposed cures of homosexuality became suspect. Although nothing changed, for some everything changed. Failure took up residence in a different home, because it was no longer welcome by those who tried to cure what they felt was a disorder. One no longer had to feel bad if he or she failed to make a homosexual into a heterosexual. Self-despair became self-congratulatory. Hope returned, and defeat disappeared.

If the normative scale or the standards that we employ in the determination of health or illness become capable of modification or change, then failure becomes relative and subject to negotiation. Indeed, it becomes more of a sociopolitical concept than a shared certainty. The slipperiness of the term demands that it be situated in a larger context that includes all the variables of the standards employed, the goals and their likelihood and/or feasibility of achievement, the method(s) employed, the competence of the therapist, the ambition of the therapist, the moment in the patient's life that may invite or reject change, along with a host of other factors peculiar to each situation.

THE INGREDIENTS FOR FAILURE

We find that our personal feelings of either hope or despair also need to become relative and subject to negotiation. We soon see that failure is a collection of a myriad of factors. Taking apart failure must consider all of the following:

1. A person (analyst or psychotherapist) who is either poorly or well trained, who
2. Employs a method competently or poorly with
3. A patient who is likely or unlikely to be affected by this method at
4. A moment in time that is propitious for this activity and that may result in
5. An endpoint that is desired by the participants and conforms to a community standard that is acceptable at that time.

Rather than allowing this complexity to dissuade one from further study, it should give us a direction to evaluate success or failure from the standpoint of a number of parameters. It was my teacher's good fortune to amass a string of successful supervisions, but it was also his misfortune to lose the opportunities to examine his failures. Replacing the nod of success and the comfort of a job well done with the shrug of failure and the discomfort of a wasted effort allows for the entrance of curiosity and even creativity. If all of your cases are successful, there is no great need to learn anything new. The satisfaction of success can well become a prison house of limited knowledge. One can only feel sympathy for the bad joke of "I have no failed cases" as well as for the linguistically challenged psychopharmacologist who insists that his patients are "treatment resistant" to his pharmacological interventions. Denial and displacement are proper areas for analysis rather than defeat.

Psychoanalysis and psychotherapy need their own pathology of treatment. Just as clinical pathology studies disease along the entire continuum from causes to signs and symptoms to whatever endpoint may occur, so too should psychoanalysis and psychotherapy turn to an examination of failed cases along the entire spectrum of error or misjudgment. Failure is not a singular event but is a manifestation of a multitude of decisions that go awry. A study of a large number of failed cases would yield no more information than one of a large number of patients with fever. In truth, many cases of infectious diseases were treated in pre-antibiotic days by vigorous efforts to reduce or eliminate the fever. Some in opposition felt that fever was a good and important feature. I cannot help but feel that many consider countertransference in a similar manner even to the point of exclaiming, "All analytic failures are due to countertransference problems."

PROPOSAL

Failure is in a sad state of neglect and is crying for an objective study. Initially, it needs to be defined. That simple task has to be done without prejudice in a spirit of inquiry rather than of blame. Failed cases need to be classified and categorized along the dimensions of the choice of treatment, the point at which the supposed failure may have occurred, the expectations of patient and therapist, as well as the competence of the therapist, which often is the least significant variable. That point needs underscoring because of this final suggestion. Every training facility and/or society should establish a scheduled regular presentation of a (properly disguised) case. Much as hospitals conduct routine "Morbidity and Mortality" meetings, analysts and therapists should present their own unsuccessful efforts in open forums of discussion. This not only is the right thing to do, but also over time may well prove to be therapeutic as well. Although the spectre of blame and responsibility routinely raises its head, only the shared community experience can over time diminish it. At this point in time, we simply do not have any idea as to the number of cases that would fail despite any effort, nor can we predict those that would do well with a minimum of effort. That seems like a good place to start.

Another reasonable suggestion that was earlier mentioned as desirable but unfeasible had to do with someone who is familiar with the variety of possible therapeutic interventions helping direct a patient to the most likely and appropriate interventions for that person. Inasmuch as that is a pie-in-the-sky hope, an alternative is possible. That consists of having the patient's history presented to a group of therapists after an initial intake interview. The group should consist of a psychotherapist, a psychopharmacologist, a psychologist familiar with CBT, and (if possible) a group therapist. Of course, this combination might be available at only some psychiatric facilities, but it may be more possible than one may think. There are always a number of imponderables operating in the assessment of any patient, but there is little doubt that most assessments are tilted in some fashion by the training and predilections of the initial interviewer. And yet it seems only fair that a decision be made following an open discussion by a group of experts exchanging their views and appraisals. In other areas of medicine, it is often true that one person is familiar with all the therapeutic possibilities for any given disorder. This is not so for much of mental illness, but our patients are no less deserving.

Inasmuch as we can never stand apart from the cases that we treat or study, we need to consider our own transferences and countertransferences to the outcomes of these cases. Our happiness at success, our disappointment at failure, and our pleasure at helping someone whom another analyst or therapist had failed to help are all part of the package that contains the result. This is not to say that patients kill themselves because we consider them untreatable or that they improve because we so want them to. Rather, it is to stress the point that we are part of the mix, and that part may also be responsible for our own failure to properly study failures. Fortunately, it is like everything else that we have learned in psychoanalysis and psychotherapy. Everything matters.

WHY DECONSTRUCTION?

The term *deconstruction* can be a bit off-putting for those unfamiliar with it and possibly equally so for those who have seen it used and misunderstood since Jacques Derrida (1985), the father of deconstruction, first began to write about it and failed to define it. For our purposes, it is meant to indicate that a word is undecidable. Especially in terms of binary opposition such as *success* and *failure*, there exists an area in which a "normal meaning" is not easily attained, and so we thereby must recognize that there is a need for a variety of meanings.

One example that comes to mind is an early control patient of mine who I thought I had successfully analyzed or at least was well on the way to successfully analyzing. An opportunity arose for him to move to another city, and, despite the feeling that more work could have and should have been done, the analysis was terminated in a manner somewhat short of ideal. I was a candidate in supervision at the time, and so this conclusion was reached with the agreement of my supervisor. I thought little more about this in the intervening years, until one day many years later a package arrived in the mail containing a letter and some photos. The letter was from my long-departed patient, and the photos were of his grandchildren. The letter was brief and primarily chatty and informative. The first comment was about the grandchildren, and the second about the fact that ever since he had been diagnosed as bipolar and placed on medication, he had been feeling fine. He sent his regards. I was dumbfounded.

Although I had felt this patient was a fairly successful analysand, I now felt puzzled. Was there any justification for even a modicum of satisfaction about this treatment? What could success or failure possibly mean if indeed the patient was bipolar? Was that diagnosis irrelevant to the analysis? Was the analysis a sham? Was my supervisor as out of touch as I? The sum and substance of my very long list of questions and the remaining state of uncertainty all seem to add up to and qualify as "undecidable."

The assignment of "undecidability" to any case requires a clear direction as to just how the decision about success or failure is to be applied. The binary coupling of the two words allows for a multitude of qualifying conditions, and so any conclusion of judgment about this particular analysis would need a preliminary statement advising one as to "how" the words are to be applied rather than just what they may mean. That *how* is the essence of deconstruction.

6

A Taxonomy of Failure

At the very first meeting of our seminar, one student in analytic training asked for a definition of a failed case, and everyone in attendance was in turn asked to offer such a definition. It soon became apparent that a major, if not fundamental, task of the group was to devise such a definition, inasmuch as many of the offered definitions were diffuse and even somewhat incoherent. Indeed, it seemed evident that what may have at one time appeared to be an obvious and even objective concept was essentially a very elusive and subjective one. Everyone had an opinion, and only a few were content with their opinions.

STARTING A CLASSIFICATION

Inasmuch as the task of placing psychoanalytic and psychodynamic failures in the straitjacket of a precise definition has proved to be elusive, it may yet be possible to form a taxonomy or systematic classification of such failures. A review of a collection of cases that are offered to the seminar on failure suggests one sort of classification (i.e., along a timeline). Of course, other kinds of groupings are feasible, but they often seem to falter because of the routine appearance of exceptions. Thus, when an effort is made to classify failure based upon the problems or pathology of a particular patient or group of patients, we often may find examples of success in the presentations of seemingly similar patients treated by other therapists. So, too, when we focus on the skills or training or theoretical bent of certain therapists, we come upon quite similar results with therapists of completely different backgrounds and competence. The problem is complicated by the one-sidedness of this or any study. Only one member of the couple is heard from. We have investigated cases that are considered to be failures by analysts and therapists, but we lack confirmatory evidence from patients. Although we did attempt to evaluate all failures from the patient's point of view, we did not interview them for their judgment.

THE TIMELINE

Suffice it to say that it is quite difficult to wrap one's arms around the idea of failure, and it offers an open invitation to a variety of unhelpful opinions. However, one cannot fail to see that progress and process are implicit in the concept of failure, and that idea naturally offers up the perspective of time. Seen as a process with a beginning, a middle, and an end allows one to consider failure as having stages, not only those that are capable of differentiation but also those that may have their own inherent difficulties. It may therefore be possible to consider phase-specific problems and their potential solutions. Indeed, one could also delineate a category of therapists or analysts who appear to do better or worse at the various stages of the treatment or analysis.

The following is a beginning approach to a taxonomy of failure based upon considering it as a process that unfolds over time. There is no intent as yet to consider what if any particular factors are peculiar to each phase or to posit any crucial accomplishment that highlights each phase. These ideas certainly merit a careful examination, which will be delayed for separate consideration. Likewise each category might well be seen in different or even opposing theoretical lights. Nevertheless, it is a start.

THE CATEGORIES

1. *Cases that never get off the ground or never seem to start*: Although these cases are focused on during the initial phase of treatment, they need not themselves be time limited. Such cases may go on and on for extended periods of time without being thought of as participating in a changeable process. Rather, they are static and may be so for the briefest time or for fairly extended periods.

2. *Cases that are interrupted and so felt to be unfinished by the therapist or analyst*: These fall into distinctly separate categories:

   A. The interruption is initiated by an external force. This force may be as follows:
      1. Interference by one or more persons who are needed in order for the treatment to continue. In children, this may be a parent. In others, it may be financial support.
      2. Unforeseen events such as a death or a job loss.

   B. Other interrupted cases can be seen as those that achieve certain changes or advances and are allowed to go no further. These interruptions can be thought of as interferences and may be as follows:
      1. The patient is feeling psychologically threatened and feels he or she must stop on his or her own.
      2. The analyst or therapist is feeling psychologically threatened and must stop.
      3. A spouse or family member is feeling psychologically threatened and insists upon a stop.

3. *Cases that go bad*: This is a distinctly separate category based upon the observation that many cases reported in a seminar devoted to studying failed cases seemed to surprise the therapist or analyst when the patient either suddenly quit or became upset and angry. Many reported

cases demonstrated an inexplicable and sudden lack of progress or a negative movement following a period that otherwise seemed without problems. Some few cases did demonstrate a very gradual deterioration after a period of progress. This observation may illustrate a shortcoming of this particular investigative effort, because perhaps not enough cases were presented to allow any sort of conclusion about prevalence. In this study, gradual deterioration was rare.

4. *Cases that go on and on without obvious improvement*: These cases are differentiated from the first category of those that never seem to benefit in that it is only in retrospect that progress seems wanting. Patient and therapist seemed lulled into a treatment that becomes more habit than movement.

5. *Cases that disappoint*: These cases are perhaps the most difficult to label because of the variability of goals assigned to psychoanalytic and dynamic psychotherapy. Expectations ordinarily become modified and altered during a treatment process, and goals are rarely clearly articulated and perhaps more rarely attained if articulated. At times both patient and therapist share their disappointment, and at times the feeling belongs to only one. The feeling of disappointment is one that usually comes at the ending of an analysis or therapy and is often tempered with thoughts of possible improvement and questionable failure. Periods of reflection on the treatment do make for an exercise in second guessing as to responsibility for failure and, at times, a resolve to do things differently if the occasion arises.

OTHER PERSPECTIVES

Before putting a high-powered lens on the particular causes of failure, it may be worthwhile to consider them from a different vantage point, one that encompasses the overall process. Just as one can study failure along a timeline, perhaps other perspectives can also be employed as well. The following is one that might be categorized as problem in the original direction of the treatment.

CASE EXAMPLE

A middle-aged divorced mother of two boys presented herself at a psychiatric clinic with the chief complaint of anxiety and depression. At one point in recording the history of this patient, she reported that she had had an unpleasant and offensive body odor for the last 30 years of her life. She had done an exhaustive study of such cases, which are representative of a syndrome termed *bromhidrosis*. There are a number of clinical reports of this particular malady along with suggestions for treatment and associated support groups. The syndrome is not classified as a psychiatric problem, but this interviewing psychiatrist could not help but consider this symptom to be something akin to a body delusion. However, this patient told of a previous visit to a psychiatric clinic in which a psychiatrist did consider her body odor to be nonexistent and attempted to disabuse her of her conviction as to its presence. She quickly left this clinic and her putative healer, never to return. The new psychiatrist decided not to pursue what he considered to be a mistaken direction and instead chose to invite the patient to participate in a course of psychotherapy. He considered the bromhidrosis to be neither a bona fide purely physical malady nor a psychiatric symptom amenable to rational discussion. Over time and with no direct mention of the symptom, its significance receded, and her initial complaint of anxiety and depression improved as well.

This case is not so much meant to be a diagnostic challenge, which it certainly is, but rather to be an interesting example of how one's initial choice of a planned course of inquiry and treatment can be crucial to success or failure. Other ways of investigating cases that may or may not be unsuccessful can and should be entertained, inasmuch as one's initial assumption about a failed case runs the risk of unwarranted closure. Another factor that is often neglected in such assessments is that of pace. Not all cases move in a regular and predictable pattern, and it is often necessary to allow oneself to become adjusted to the rhythm of a case before delivering a judgment as to its treatability. However, the footnote to that caution is a warning that sometimes rhythms change in unpredictable fashions. The other major warning has to do with cases that by all means of measure are truly untreatable.

UNTREATABLE CASES

At first blush, it may seem that untreatable cases and failed cases are coexistent. Yet it is important to recognize that this is not always true. Our study, which we shall more fully describe, discovered that trained therapists could not agree on either category; some cases felt to be failures by some were not so designated by others, and some cases called untreatable by some were not felt to be so by others. And these two groups were markedly different groups. Despite the vagueness of the very concept of failure, at times a case does seem to be clearly untreatable.

CASE EXAMPLE

A young married woman described by her therapist as "gorgeous and fascinating" but who also turned out to be a very high-priced prostitute was presented to our seminar as a failed case. The chief complaint of this possible patient was of impulsive behavior and what the therapist termed *hypomania*. This latter term was attributed to activity involving an abortion, the sale of her engagement and wedding rings, and sleeping with an ex-boyfriend.

Early on in the therapy, which consisted of a combination of medication and psychotherapy, the patient began to miss sessions because of oversleeping. The therapist changed the treatment schedule to accommodate this problem, which, however, did not abate. The therapist felt that his goal was "to make a connection" with the patient, and he felt that he was somewhat successful as over time she got divorced and began a new relationship with a new man. However, she soon decided to go to Paris to once again take up prostitution and left owing money to the therapist.

The ensuing discussion focused upon the question of "patient-hood" and whether or not this patient met the minimal criteria for this state. Some said that as long as someone comes voluntarily for the relief of subjective distress, he or she should be considered a patient. The additional information that the patient was involved in a custody battle over her 2½-year-old son and was required to seek therapy was not initially available, but this fact seemed to have little impact on the group's evaluation of her treatability.

All in all, most members of the seminar felt that this case merited classification as a failure, with one or two claiming the patient had been helped. The majority, however, added that the patient was hardly ever a "real" patient and should also be classified as untreatable. In contrast to patients who "drop out" of therapy, she had attended a total of 34 sessions and had received a variety of psychotropic medications. She appears to be nicely representative of cases that qualify for a failure with an open question as to whether she had ever become a patient.

One factor in the determination of the status of failure is that of the conviction of the therapist as to whether or not he or she has failed. This conclusion is reached only if one has made an initial assumption that some sort of goal may be achieved. The fact that this particular therapist described his patient as "gorgeous and fascinating" easily leads one to believe that a less alluring woman may have more quickly attained the ranking of untreatable and thereby completely avoided being labeled as a failed case. The particular rescue fantasies that allow one to pursue a challenge that someone else may either initially or fairly quickly abandon are the crucial ingredients in the determination and differentiation of assignment of untreatability. What may not have been initially evident soon became eminently clear to us: Failure is always a mutual construction. One person's failure is often another person's opportunity.

CLASSIFICATION OF CAUSES

If one momentarily puts to the side the examination of when a failure occurs, the misdirection of a case, the pace of a case, or even the basic untreatability of a case, the most significant issue to be studied about failed cases is the answer to the question of just why it happened. The parallel question to this is, of course, "Could it have been prevented in some manner?"

In our study of failed cases, we devised a rating sheet that referred to most of the issues discussed in terms of the timeline for failure as well as our search for a better definition of failure. We asked that cases be evaluated on both objective and subjective scales of failure for both therapist and patient. Of course, we would need a large sample of cases to make any definitive judgment about time, and we would need careful follow-up patient interviews as to objective evidence (e.g., was there concrete evidence for change along with subjective; and did the therapist and patient feel much had been accomplished?). Nevertheless, our small sample of 25–30 cases revealed a surprising amount of agreement that led to the tentative conclusion that cases failed with not much relevance to the length of time that was involved in the treatment. Also, most of the presenters and listeners agreed as to the effectiveness of the treatment. The major variation in the ratings seemed to be around a diehard conviction for some that no treatment was a complete failure. This would appear to partially account for the continuing problem of definition. It is very difficult for some to acknowledge and grapple with the idea of failure, and so we began to open a window on an approach to asking the right questions.

The questions that we asked had to do with the likely causes, which we have enumerated in Chapter 2 and shall list below, for a case failure. The reasons were to be ruled as primary, secondary, or tertiary so as not to force our raters to determine a single cause. It may or may not come as a surprise that our participant could best agree on the least likely cause for failure rather than the most likely. The causes that were offered for their selection were as follows:

1. *Lack of knowledge*: This started our list, because our cases came from a wide group of psychotherapists and analysts with varied background and training. Thus, we wondered if it may have been felt that one simply was ill equipped to pursue the treatment of what turned out to be difficult cases. A majority of our responders felt this was not a very significant issue and rated it as least likely.

2. *Lack of empathy and lack of a sustained empathic state*: We divided this scale into two parts because there appeared to be a difference in those patients who were able to make a good initial connection with the analyst or therapist and those who could not maintain the connection over time. Although only a slight statistical difference in the two was noted, the variation will be pursued in later chapters (e.g., see Chapters 13 and 14) in an effort to explain the conviction that this is the area of major countertransference problems.

3. *Using alternative approaches*: The vagueness of this category was meant to cover everything from medication to CBT to other forms of psychotherapy to other theoretical approaches to psychoanalysis. Our raters did not seem to think that failing to employ an alternative approach was tantamount to not knowing how to employ an alternative approach, because over half of them agreed that this neglect of application was responsible for the failure. However, they rarely named the alternative. They seemed to embrace the idea that something else might have done the trick, although they did not pinpoint just what that something else was or how to use it.

Perhaps the lingering hope that no case is a failure allows for the choice of some other approach. However, a substantial majority of the raters did consider a good number of cases as being fundamentally untreatable.

This brief overview of our seminar and its results is meant to do
no more than introduce a problem and to suggest further lines of
inquiry. No large-scale empirical study is possible unless and until
a number of issues are initially clarified, and it remains an open
question as to whether any study could reach reasonable conclusions about failure without a clear agreement on what the term
means. One comment on the problem directed our attention to
suicide as a clear-cut indicator of failure. It is instructive to compare the methods used by general psychiatry to employ the terms
success and *failure*. A standard textbook on psychopharmacology (Janicak et al., 2006) assesses treatment success by asking the
patient about symptoms or, for more seriously disturbed patients,
by interviewing family or nursing personnel about the behavior of
the patient. Most studies of the efficacy of the treatment of borderline personality disorder rely on the frequency of suicide attempts
and the need for hospitalization in order to gauge the success or
failure of a treatment (Bateman & Fonagy, 2008). Some employ
a scale that evaluates symptoms and general adaptation. For the
most part, the aim is for objectivity based upon patient reports
and observable behavior. However, one author (Rosenblatt, 2010)
stressed greater social, marital, and vocational functioning as
good outcome indicators and thus moved beyond easily measurable features. The search for objective, observable, or measurable
parameters does not usually involve anything approaching the
subjective opinion of the therapist and his or her contribution in
the evaluation.

Because our perspective on failure insists upon the contributions of both patient and therapist, the issues to be pursued are
those involving the formulation of goals, the ability to attain
and sustain a workable connection, the differences in therapist
contribution in terms of a theoretical guide, and primarily just
what failure means to each member of the constructed unit. All
of our case presenters are, of course, strikingly different from the

psychopharmacologist who administers a medication and attributes the results to the drug. Compliance to the directions for the drug may be a psychological problem, but once ingested the effects are drug dependent, and the prescriber is removed from the equation. We felt it very important to include the analyst or psychotherapist as part of the study, and all were interviewed after presentation. Both participating in treatment and telling others about the treatment are important elements in our understanding of failure. The ability of some psychiatrists to assess patients as "treatment resistant" (Brent et al., 2009) is stark testimony to the wish of these psychiatrists to become invisible and so to eliminate all personal responsibility for their failures. What follows is a totally different pursuit.

7

Failure to Launch

Some cases in psychotherapy as well as in psychoanalysis seem never to get off the ground. Despite the recognition of the need for a clear establishment of a therapeutic or working alliance and regardless of the theory behind these concepts (Levy, 2000), there seems to be some added ingredient that needs to be necessary to effect change or merely to initiate movement in treatment. In contrast to some patients who are what we may call *changeable* are those who may well form a comfortable relationship with therapists, come regularly and on time, and pay their fee promptly and correctly, yet nothing much seems to happen. Indeed, these arrangements of convenience and comfort may persist for extended periods of time, yet with no discernable alteration in the status quo. Some therapists describe such arrangements as "paid companionships," and some defend such arrangements as offering opportunities for patients to express their emotions or reveal hidden thoughts. There may even be arguments over whether it is proper to consider these static enterprises as therapy or analysis, and especially so if one should attribute the concept of assigning failure to an activity that hardly actually failed, because it never really developed a clearly defined goal of any kind. Rather like the missile that never leaves the ground, these treatments failed only to launch, only to start what should be a process.

No attempt will be made here to distinguish this form of failure from that of not forming a therapeutic or working alliance. Some of the patients to be presented for consideration may qualify as being unable or unwilling to join with a therapist or analyst in the special form of inquiry that is considered to be a sine qua non for an analysis. Some may be characterized as quite eager to cooperate in such a venture. No doubt, one could claim the absence of the hoped-for alliance in many of these cases, but they range from the most recalcitrant patient to the most cooperative and still share this characteristic of nonachievement or of not making even a beginning to change.

I propose to present a series of case vignettes in order to differentiate several categories of patients who exhibit an inability or reluctance to pursue a course of psychotherapy or psychoanalysis. Although these patients may appear to be quite dissimilar in their initial presentations and subsequent behavior, they do all share this fundamental feature of what is best seen as a failure to begin and pursue treatment. They do, however, differ in a number of other respects that merit attention.

CASE EXAMPLE

Tom was referred to a psychoanalyst following his release from a residential treatment facility where he had lived for a few months while he worked in a job as a lab technician at a nearby pharmaceutical company. He was said to be in psychotherapy during his time in this treatment center and was eager to resume it with a new therapist. His past psychiatric history was a complex one with frequent changes of therapists and some short periods of hospitalization. Tom met his new therapist and appeared to immediately hit it off with him. This therapist felt a good connection with his patient and later commented on how much they seemed to like one another. When describing this patient to a consultant, the analyst was embarrassed about the fact that he had learned little of the patient's past history other than a brief description of his parents, who were characterized as being unreliable caretakers.

Tom and his therapist set a schedule for Tom's treatment, and Tom rather quickly disregarded it. Although he did occasionally call to cancel an appointment, he just as often either came quite late or did not show up at all. The therapist sought consultation with no apparent helpful advice, and soon thereafter Tom called to say he might prefer a female therapist. He was referred and was not heard from again. A call to the potential next therapist revealed that Tom had not made contact.

This case primarily serves to highlight a common problem in all forms of therapy (i.e., the dropout rate). This can probably be thought of essentially as a failure to adequately launch a treatment regardless of its particular form and frequency. A recent article on the comparison of forms of treatment for borderline personality disorder (Doering et al., 2010) noted dropout rates as high as 67.3% in some forms of therapy and as low as 25% in others. This lower rate was noted in countries where psychotherapy was offered at no cost to patients, but when compared to fee-based treatment it grew to close to 60% (Doering et al., 2010, p. 393). The dropout rate is arbitrarily chosen to be measured at some convenient point in time and so may well differ from a measurement reflecting a failure to begin treatment successfully, but in all likelihood these are patients who are not able to form a working alliance or are not equipped with whatever mysterious ingredient that is needed to become a patient who is helped. They drop out before anything happens, although dropout rates are computed near the onset of a planned therapy. The timeline for the determination of a failure to actively engage in psychoanalysis or psychotherapy is often somewhat of a surprise.

CASE EXAMPLE

Dr. S. presented a report of a patient of his whom he had been seeing for 10 years with no appreciable change in her initial symptoms of despair and suicidality. Dr. S. was at his wit's end as to both his past and his future care of this patient. He felt that nothing whatsoever had been accomplished with his patient, although she continued to regularly come. Although she often missed an appointment, she by no means appeared to look or act the part of an uncommitted patient, although Dr. S. insisted there had been no movement whatsoever in this supposed treatment.

The patient had earlier announced her plan to suicide when her daughter finished high school, and Dr. S. felt this was a sincere and determined decision on her part. He said her sessions were filled with only casual conversation, and he reported that rarely was anything "personal" discussed.

The participants in the case presentation took exception to the idea that a patient of 10 years could be considered to be one who had never really participated in treatment. All sorts of explanations were offered ranging from the suggestion that the treatment, as it were, had kept the patient from suicide on to the problem lying with the therapist's countertransference or perhaps his limitations as to technique. Dr. S. left the conference with the conviction that this remained an inexplicable failure. In contrast to the perhaps uncertain status of this case are those that seem strikingly clear as to this particular form of a failure.

The difference between the first two cases is one that turns attention upon the therapist and his role in the case failure. Our first therapist insisted that Tom and Tom alone brought about the lack of a treatment process. On the other hand, Dr. S. felt puzzled as to his personal impact on this prolonged course of treatment with no recognizable impact. Could he have done something differently? Was there something that he simply did not comprehend? Before seeing Dr. S., this patient had had several unsuccessful efforts at treatment, so Dr. S. was convinced that at a minimum he had managed to keep his patient in treatment, if indeed it could be called that. Our next case continues the effort to place responsibility.

CASE EXAMPLE

Linda came to see a psychoanalyst on the advice of the therapist of the man with whom she had been involved for approximately

13 years. She and her paramour, Fred, were living together and had been talking about marriage for several years. One day, she had returned unexpectedly to their apartment from a business trip to find Fred entertaining another couple along with a woman he was escorting. Linda was furious and stormed out of the apartment, which she felt was jointly hers. Fred followed with pleas and apologies. Over time, Fred managed to placate Linda with a variety of psychological explanations offered by his therapist. As a part of the effort to effect a happy reconciliation, it was suggested that Linda see a therapist primarily in order to better understand Fred. The referral to Dr. B. was chosen by Fred's therapist, and Linda went to see him without much conviction as to ameliorating the situation.

In the first meeting with Dr. B., Linda reported both the painful encounter noted above with Fred and his guests along with the history of the painful lengthy affair with an uncommitted Fred. To the best of his memory, Dr. B. later reflected on the hour with the possibility that perhaps he had displayed overdue sympathy at Linda's plight. In the second hour, Linda continued her tale of other unreliable men with whom she had had lengthy relationships and also announced that she was angry and upset at something Dr. B. had said about the nature of her involvements. This negative comment troubled Dr. B., who could not remember having said much at all, but who later noted to himself that he did feel that Linda was somehow allowing herself to be mistreated. Linda seemed to end this second hour on a positive note. She later called to cancel her next scheduled appointment. After a few bills were sent to her, she settled her account and was not heard from again.

Dr. B. thought about the failure of this case to get off the ground and decided that Linda needed to turn her passively induced injury into an active one by dumping her potential therapist just as she had felt unceremoniously dumped by her boyfriend. However, another possibility occurred to him in terms of his evaluation of Linda as a poor soul who allowed herself to be abused. The last thing Linda had said as she was preparing to leave Dr. B.'s office was to ask Dr. B. if he thought it wise for her to see Fred's therapist. Dr. B. responded by saying that he could see no reason for her to do so. Now Dr. B. wondered if he had unwittingly communicated his contempt for her submissive posture. Could he have behaved otherwise? Would Linda have done better with another therapist or with a female therapist? Although there are presently unanswered questions, they do require some confrontations as to the possibilities. All cases that fail to participate in a reasonable course of treatment can be either dismissed or worried over. They deserve a careful unpacking inasmuch as they pose another possible category of failure to launch.

CASE EXAMPLE

Dr. D. sensed an instant dislike in the first encounter with his new patient, Leonard. He later could describe a variety of things about Leonard that aroused such antipathy in him ranging from his slovenly appearance to his reluctance to saying much of anything. Leonard had been urged to see Dr. D. because a friend had insisted that he do so, but Leonard felt the problem with his friend had little to do with himself. However, he had acquiesced to a psychological evaluation in spite of this feeling. Thus, he had little to say to Dr. D. other than the resentment he had at being put in an uncomfortable position.

As Dr. D. and Leonard began to talk, it did become clear that Leonard had reason enough to seek psychiatric help but was loath to confront the evidence for it. This evidence ranged from a good deal of dishonesty and deceptiveness in Leonard's life to a variable dissatisfaction on Leonard's part with the life he was leading. On the particular day of this first interview with Dr. D., the level of dissatisfaction was minimal and the combination of this with the negative attributes of Leonard's life added up to a further negative appraisal of Leonard as a likely patient by Dr. D.

Although Leonard did come for a second visit with Dr. D., things went no more smoothly than during the first visit, and the two concluded on a note of uncertainty. That is to say that Leonard agreed to think about entering psychotherapy, but to no surprise of Dr. D. he never made another appointment, much to Dr. D.'s relief.

When asked to reconsider the case of Leonard, Dr. D. had no reluctance to recognize his personal dislike of his prospective patient, but he insisted that he had effectively concealed these feelings during the interview. However, Dr. D. did confess that the prospect of a lengthy relationship with Leonard did dismay him, and thus Leonard's disappearance from his professional life was met with relief. He further suggested the real possibility that perhaps Leonard would have been more successfully handled by another therapist.

RECAPITULATION

The above cases range from one that appears to portend a failure from the very onset due to the particular nature of the patient, on to the somewhat questionable or equivocal likelihood of failure that might characterize those cases that could succeed or fail because of qualities of both therapist and patient. It is an interesting exercise in the problem of psychopathology to attempt to position or locate the difficulty of a successful treatment. As we move from one case to the next, we can note the contribution of the therapist in terms of a working match or a mismatch. It is relatively easy to insist upon suspending a conclusion about pathology until one can assess the intersubjective issue (i.e., the relationship determines the nature of both the difficulty and the solution). It may be obvious that the final case involved a therapist who could not readily connect with his patient, and so one could entertain the possibility of another therapist doing a better job. Of course, one could imagine that almost any therapist would have a similar reaction to this particular patient and so situate the problem in this patient's capacity to evoke a sense of defeat in almost any other therapist. Patients should not be thought of as closed-off entities but rather as open systems with a changeable ecosystem. As such, it may well be the case that no particular patient can be evaluated outside of the inclusion and reckoning of the person doing the evaluation. Yet it may seem foolhardy to propose that the first patient presented in this chapter could be captured as a patient in the presence of a different therapist, just as the last patient might have charmed a quite different therapist.

An intersubjective viewpoint often seems to suggest an equal contribution from each participant, whereas a focus on one or the other person tends to assign full responsibility to either patient or therapist. Another point of view sees the degree of involvement on a continuum. Perhaps some patients require a great deal of involvement by a therapist, whereas others can make it with almost anyone with but a minimum of participation. Along this line of the active or inactive role of a therapist, our first patient might conceivably be well served by someone, and the same may be so of all of the case examples.

Only a theoretical perspective that includes the role and presence of the other is capable of explaining the discrepancies in this initial effort to launch treatment. Added to this is the inevitable question about analysis or therapy making a significant alteration in the patient. Seen along the line of making a difference, the inability of some patients to undergo a meaningful treatment calls for a distinction between patients who cannot merely start from those who can start as long as they need not move. Thus, the failure to launch a treatment should include an assessment of the role of the therapist as an "other" of understanding versus one of both understanding coupled with alteration. The role of the "other" can indeed be a necessary factor in patients for whom an empathic connection is salutary, whereas it can be seen as threatening for those for whom breaks in empathy cannot be endured. Of course, there are other ways to think about these two categories of patients. At times, there may be a reasonable distinction made between supportive therapy and a more dynamic approach. This difference can even be said to describe how one approach such as support may gradually over time lead to more active or interpretive work that evolves into a more dynamic interaction. However, there is no denying the existence of patients who, with the cooperation of the therapist, seem to go nowhere.

CASE EXAMPLE

Bernard called to make an appointment with Dr. E. after the death of his mother. He had had a number of previous experiences in psychotherapy and announced at the start of his encounter with Dr. E. that he did not wish to get into the "way back to childhood machine," nor did he wish to have any of his dreams interpreted. Dr. E. did not protest, and over time they discussed Bernard's relationship with his mother and the complicated handling of the mother's estate. Bernard seemed to like coming to see Dr. E. and never failed to arrange a substitute appointment if he was forced to miss a regularly scheduled one. Dr. E. made one or two attempts to talk about Bernard's developmental history along with several efforts to discuss one or two dreams that Bernard offered with the clear proviso that he had no interest or wish for these dreams to be decoded. On a few occasions, Bernard commented on the cost of his so-called treatment, but he never seemed to contemplate ending it, all the while insisting that it did not matter very much. However, he may have said that it did not matter without any corresponding feeling as to its insignificance. Occasionally, he cautioned Dr. E. not to mention certain issues that he said might depress him.

Bernard was not unaware of his obvious resistance to undergoing the (for him) routine process of dynamic therapy, and Dr. E. assumed that his previous therapy had been traumatic. However, over time, he was disabused of that assumption as the few references to his several other therapists seemed to confirm that they differed little from the role assigned to Dr. E. After a few sessions, Dr. E. and Bernard seemed to drift into some sort of "steady state" that consisted of friendly reports ranging from birdwatching expeditions to visits to the urologist or dermatologist. But not much more.

Although some may say that Bernard's continued attendance in regular appointments qualified him to be considered in treatment and indeed indicated that he was benefiting from treatment, Dr. E. often felt otherwise. Compared to the suicidal patient described in this chapter who had been seen for over 10 years by Dr. S., there was no hint of real concern about Bernard. Compared to the suicidal patient, there was no impetus for change on the part of either patient or therapist. Certainly the nature of the connection between these patients and their therapists was quite different. The relative comfort that characterized the relationship between Dr. E. and Bernard was strikingly different from the ongoing tension and concern that were ever-present companions of Dr. S. Yet they were also the same. Both Dr. E. and Dr. S. felt a strong connection to their patients, and this connection was echoed by the patients. They also shared a quite significant similarity in that each patient made it clear that they would not, or perhaps could not, move. They thus seemed to qualify as belonging to the "failure-to-launch" group, and to evoke questions as to exactly where one might locate the problem or the pathology. Perhaps the therapists were seduced into a certain attitude of complacency, or perhaps these patients represent a rigid resistance to change that essentially reflects an insistence that any change is inadvisable.

Essentially Dr. E. could readily rationalize the static nature of Bernard's treatment by noting the overall comfort of both patient and therapist. He readily endorsed a position of therapy being meaningful only if someone is uncomfortable, and so he insisted that his patient could not tolerate the discomfort. No matter that ultimately treatment should result in an overall feeling of well-being, the road to that final state was a road of difficulty. No doubt different theoretical approaches (Bacal, 1985) would challenge this assumption, but Dr. E. felt that the lack of pain reflected a lack of progress. Later the theory that directed Dr. E.'s ideas will be further elaborated (Chapter 15), but regardless of the possible intertheoretical differences Bernard appeared to be unchanged. Some might say that that need not reflect failure. This perhaps highlights not only differences in theory but also differences in the very definition of failure.

There seem to be two distinct groups to be differentiated. The first is unable to form and sustain a connection, one that goes under a variety of names ranging from a *relationship*, a *therapeutic* or *working alliance*, a *selfobject union*, and so on. The failure to form such a connection may lie with either the patient or the therapist, and here is where the work on a proper match (Kantrowitz, 1995) is relevant. Once formed, this connection must be sustained, and this has become an area much in need of investigation, inasmuch as it leads into one's consideration of the second group. This consists of patients who seem unable to endure and profit from some sort of disruption in the connection. The disruption also is noted under a variety of names ranging from *undoing repression* to *developmental growth* to *empathic break*, and the like. By no means are these phrases meant to be equivalent, but they merely indicate the different ways the process of therapy may be conceptualized. Essentially, the effort is directed at altering the status quo; some patients do this well, and some not at all.

THE RELATIONSHIP AND ITS FATE

There can be no denial of the positive and beneficial effects of an effective relationship. It allows many patients to feel both integrated and understood. Much is made of the ameliorative role of an empathic bond, and much is said to result from its continued operation, although it often goes under a variety of names. Some entire theoretical yields are posited on the efforts directed toward the establishment and therapeutic work of that "relationship" (Mitchell, 1988). Much has also been written and critiqued in terms of the abuse of the relationship or empathic bond (Gabbard, 1994). The crucial factor appears to lie in the connection or bond remaining static. Some of these established albeit unchanging

relationships reflect what may be seen as a "supportive therapeutic relationship" and so reflect a positive result of treatment.
As such, many treatments do not progress much beyond these
points and should not need to do so. The failure or reluctance to
move beyond these stable positions may lie in the pathology of the
patient, the psychology of the therapist, or the limitations of the
theory that is underscoring the treatment. The attribution of failure is applicable to such states if an alteration in these connections
is both desirable and possible.

It seems appropriate to conceptualize those treatments that
attain and maintain a static state as evidencing a failure of sorts.
Of course, this appellation should only apply if stasis reflects a
less desirable position in someone who could move to a condition
that reflects whatever is thought to be closer to an optimum state
of health. A good example of this issue is seen in self psychology,
which posits a sequence of (a) the establishment of an empathic
bond, followed by (b) an empathic break that is or should be occa-
sioned by one or more interpretations, leading to (c) a manageable
traumatic state created by the break in empathy, resulting in (d) a
buildup of psychic structure and the correlative (e) internalized
relation to a more enduing selfobject union, a capacity for self-
reflection, and a better feeling of self-integration. Of course, these
are able to be seen as fanciful theoretical descriptions, and there
is no doubt that different theoretical approaches would offer other
forms of explanation, but the single fundamental point is that of
movement and change. Failure to launch is a failure to promote a
move regardless of the ability to create a condition of comfort and
a feeling of being understood.

The patients who are described range from those who fail to get
beyond a few initial appointments to those who maintain a continued and regular attendance. Some represent immediate dissatisfaction, and others lasting contentment, but none seem to
change very much. The early dropouts can be considered to be
untreatable no matter the therapist, whereas the lasting ones can

be considered as enjoying a continuing sense of support. Yet both groups demand our attention as a form of failure unless the goal is that of mere attendance.

Cases of failure to launch open a line of investigation of failure as one of a continuing process of change and movement. Thus, they ask for investigation and scrutiny of those that fail to start, those that have a positive movement interrupted, and those that end badly. Interruptions can come from outside forces or from unforeseen events. Endings can occur badly from disappointments that are dramatic or from those that are subtle but fall short of the initial formulation of goals. These sometimes occur after a period of promise or one of stagnation. However, all failure offers an opportunity for learning. We should begin with the very fundamental point of the exact nature of an empathic bond, a topic of Chapter 13.

8

Interruptions, Interferences, and Bad Endings

One early sign of a failed case that emerged during our seminars review was one mentioned in Chapter 3, a surprise of the presenting analyst or therapist when the case suddenly and inexplicably went bad. Inasmuch as our conference was planned as a beginning inquiry into the nature of failed cases, we initially did not give much weight to this occurrence, and only when a series of such events presented themselves did we begin to wonder what the possible meaning of this surprise might be.

INTERRUPTIONS

The similarity of a number of these cases was striking in that there was a rather common series of events. The analysis or treatment began with a variety of problems that focused on either the fee or the schedule. The patient did not quickly settle into any sort of routine of performance but rather became involved in a number of extra-analytic activities ranging from affairs to marital arguments to job changes. The analyst noted his or her distance from the patient and/or felt a certain lack of commitment on the part of the patient. Most of the interruptions happened to occur around the time of an announced vacation by the analyst with one or two exceptions involving a necessary leave taking by the patient. After these separations, the patient would briefly return only to announce a plan to quit the treatment. There was a uniform reaction of shock or dismay on the part of the therapist, who then became preoccupied with what is termed *soul searching*. The quest was for an answer to the sense of personal blame, a feeling of having done something wrong, and/or a conviction of having ruined a possibly successful analysis or psychotherapy. This was regularly followed by a number of explanations that usually settled on the untreatability of the patient. The primary error or mistake made by the therapist or analyst was that of optimism as to the potential of this patient to be analyzed or treated successfully. A conviction of having made a bad choice allowed us the relief of absolution, which was, however, often short-lived.

There existed a certain uniformity of feeling among both presenters and listeners that these were *not* cases that never really got started. All felt a feeling of a process that was begun and disrupted along with a modicum of disappointment. This latter feeling is the best indicator of a more meaningful relationship than that seen in our cases that fail to launch. It is a barometer of a connection, an empathic union that is always dialectic, and so the disruption is a mutual experience. We shall later discuss the particular meanings of empathic unions in all psychotherapy and psychoanalysis, but now merely note how it may serve to distinguish one case of failure from another. The feeling of the break in empathy will become a guidepost to enable us to evaluate interrupted cases as those that have established an empathic connection as opposed as those that have not, as well as to examine the reasons for and the result of such empathic breaks.

One suggestion that was offered, but could not easily be confirmed, is that these patients who discontinued were fearful of enduring a more significant disruption and so brought about one that they could themselves control. One patient told his analyst that he felt better during her vacation (i.e., when he was away from analysis than in her presence). He insisted on the absence of missing her or of longing for her return. He thus became the active master of a potentially traumatic experience. The oft-noted remark "This patient was not really in analysis (or treatment)" was not heard during the discussion of interrupted cases, but the query as to what else could have been done or what went wrong was a common one.

INTERFERENCES

Compared to the shock and surprise of an interrupted case, those that demonstrated a clear source of interference usually were characterized as recognizing and being aware of a potential danger to the treatment before its actual occurrence. The most blatant of these interferences seem to implicitly declare themselves at the very onset of the treatment and are often not fully recognized as to their potential impact.

CASE EXAMPLE

This middle-aged married mother of three entered analysis primarily on the urging of the analyst of her husband, who referred her to this younger analyst. The husband had been in analysis for quite some time, and both he and his analyst felt that the persistent marital troubles called for both parties to be in treatment. The presenting analyst had only recently graduated from his analytic training and felt pleased and honored to be chosen by an older teacher to treat the wife of his patient.

This course of treatment was not a brief one, but it suffered an unexpected and somewhat startling termination. Suffice it to say that this analysis appeared to effect a number of changes in this patient's life save for the continuing difficulties with the husband, whose behavior was felt as both difficult and intractable by both the patient and *her* analyst. She began to recognize that the continuation of her marriage to this man was in conflict with her own growth and development, and so she also began to contemplate the possibility of a divorce. Her analyst was quite able to join her in this consideration, but admitted to his personal misgivings about the possible reaction of the admired referring analyst.

Arguments ensued between the patient and her husband, with him accusing her of getting nothing from her treatment and ultimately demanding that she stop. He himself was planning to terminate his own rather lengthy analysis and said that he could not fathom her alone being in analysis. The contemplation of divorce frightened the patient, and the suggestion that the two consider some sort of couple's therapy was vetoed by the husband's analyst. Once again, the woman's analyst felt the presence of the husband's analyst in his consulting room along with that of the patient and her spouse. Finally, the patient announced that she felt it necessary to stop her treatment in order to continue with her marriage. The analyst felt he had failed.

Some of the cases of interference are more subtle than others, but essentially the treatment does seem to ever involve another person or persons demanding acknowledgment and so preventing the working through of the problem with the analyst or therapist. This unseen presence of the other is regularly experienced in the treatment of children with the parental influence demonstrating itself in the form of actual meetings, regular phone calls, or payment problems. However, some third parties are much more in the background even to the point of supposed invisibility and total anonymity. This is best exemplified by the supervisor who is either required or requested by many therapists and analytic candidates.

There is a large literature on the role of the supervisor in psychotherapy and psychoanalysis (Fleming & Benedek, 1983), with the usual emphasis on both its helpfulness and its necessity. Some reports of failed cases, however, reveal ongoing disagreements and conflicts between student and teacher as to how best to handle and understand the case material. This often happens if the supervisor and therapist are wedded to different theoretical persuasions, but can also occur if there are more fundamental problems in learning. From the supervisor who insisted on sitting in the corner during an analytic session (Goldberg, 2010) to the one who equates supervision with therapy (Fleming & Benedek, 1983), many therapists cannot free themselves from this feeling of being watched, evaluated, and criticized. Of course, there are a host of possible outside interferences in any treatment, and they range from helpful to harmful, but at times the only possible resolution of a conflict is the discontinuation of the treatment. It is when the disparity in power from status and position leads to an impasse that we often find a failed case becomes the only answer.

Several cases were reported that showed evidence of the interfering supervisor with some few ending with the student changing the supervisor and others ending with the failure of the case. What was missing from these case reports was what may appear obvious from one point of view, and that is the use of a consultant to serve as arbitrator or mediator. Probably this is rare or unusual because of the power differential. Nevertheless, the patient is often an unwitting bystander in a conflict similar to the case noted in this chapter, in which the power problem led to the junior analyst's position as a helpless onlooker.

The problem with an accurate evaluation of an interfered case is often that of settling for one goal over another. Just as one might feel that the patient in the aforementioned case was surely somewhat better off as a result of the treatment, so too might it be necessary to modify and alter one's goals as a treatment progresses. That sort of flexibility allows one to cast interference in a new light, inasmuch as it can be considered as a limit-setting move that takes into account the larger system in which patient and therapist operate. This form of a larger perspective is also needed in educational systems as well.

We shall have an extended discussion of goals in Chapter 12, but it is necessary for us to recognize that goals are often implicit rather than explicit. A perfectionistic attitude can be as much of an impediment to success as one that is overly casual. Much of the problem in the definition of failure is the vagueness of the goal of the treatment, which is not only difficult to articulate but also often impossible to achieve. The best example of this is that of the student referred for treatment because she could not pass her French exam to qualify for a PhD. The treatment soon revealed that her own personal goal was never to get a PhD, for reasons that came out in her treatment.

BAD ENDINGS

There are no reliable data on the incidence of happy endings in psychotherapy or psychoanalysis. Many treatments end from unpredictable factors that may be welcomed in a treatment that may be seen as unending. Some end from mutual exhaustion, and some from a planned moment in time. One immediate distinction in the categorization of endings is those that are based on some internal sense of the patient versus those that are based on an external and visible point of reference. The patient who came to treatment because she could not learn French did not reach her particular endpoint of passing her language requirement for a PhD but rather came to an internal sense of preferring an entirely different career choice.

Once a termination is brought up as the central issue in an ongoing treatment, the entire course of the treatment is altered. Unforeseen factors such as a death or a geographical change do not allow for the particular experience felt to be peculiar to the termination phase and so are representative of bad endings in therapy. We should define a *bad ending* as one that occurs in an otherwise successful treatment and so becomes something like the hallmark of the treatment that may otherwise have been a success.

CASE EXAMPLE

Peter was a man involved in an unhappy marriage that he felt was the product of a long-standing and rocky affair from which he could not extricate himself. He felt that he could not enter into marital therapy because his wife was unaware of his infidelity and so came to individual psychotherapy as a last resort.

Peter did quite well in treatment, and over time his marriage improved. Much to Peter's surprise, his paramour became discontented with their illicit relationship and unilaterally decided to break it off. There was a good deal of arguing and contention over the ending of this affair, which was finalized only by the bitter departure of the spurned lover. The therapist was himself pleased with this turn of affairs and felt that he and his patient could now begin to consider termination. However, Peter just disappeared. He paid his bill. He called to cancel his appointments. He was seen no more.

Peter's therapist went to a consultant to better understand what may have gone wrong in an otherwise well-managed and seemingly successful case, or, perhaps better said, a potentially successful case. What had he done wrong, and what might he have done differently? After a cursory review of Peter's history along with the details of the treatment, the consultant merely nodded and said that Peter seemed committed to bad endings. He could not end his illicit affair or his marriage, and so certainly he could not manage a good ending to his treatment. The case was not a failure but an accurate portrayal of Peter's way of handling things. His therapist felt pleased and absolved of guilt, and everything ended on a good note.

It is important to recognize that there is no blueprint for ending psychotherapy or psychoanalysis. Some do it one way, and some another. There may well be an ideal way to conduct a termination, but as with many ideals it may not be realized. Like with so many other issues that characterize treatment, the subjective element becomes the crucial one. There is no doubt that Peter would describe his therapy as successful, and little doubt that he would think very much was askew about the ending. His therapist retained a normative scheme of treatment as a guide to it being a success or failure. No doubt, most bad endings cannot be as easily resolved as that of Peter.

CASE EXAMPLE

A therapist presents a case that he felt clearly ended badly with the patient leaving vile and angry messages on his voice mail and the therapist feeling that he had extended himself as much as humanly possible with this patient. He had seen him over an extended period of time and had allowed frequent phone calls and voice mails whenever the patient felt lonely or unhappy. He had also prescribed a variety of medications for the patient that had been helpful.

The patient had described a history of growing up with unhappy parents who divorced when he was quite young. The treatment seemed to center on a series of unsuccessful relationships with women with whom he usually stopped seeing after discovering faults that ranged from too much feeling to not enough feeling. The therapist at one time offered to go running with his patient, and so at least one hour per week was devoted to this mutual activity. In his presentation of the case, the therapist focused upon his efforts to make and sustain an empathic connection with his patient along with his continued concern that perhaps more running or other forms of treatment such as cognitive-behavioral therapy (CBT) would be useful. There was little doubt that the therapist was quite devoted to the patient as well as troubled that he was not doing enough. At one point, the therapist told the patient that he had not provided to the patient all that was needed. He told the group that he felt the patient was asking for the impossible. At last, the patient asked to come only once per month; when the therapist disagreed, the patient cancelled all future appointments. Shortly after that, the angry messages began.

A cloud of disappointment hung over the telling of this tale as well as the later discussion. The patient was disappointed in his mother and father, who were obviously disappointed with one another. All of his relationships were fraught with disappointment, and this extended to his therapist, who initially seemed determined on not disappointing the patient but who ultimately succumbed to what appeared to be inevitable. The rage that ended this treatment seemed almost fitting in that the treatment expressed a hope and promise that could not be fulfilled. The extra efforts made by the therapist up to and including going for runs with the patient were vivid portrayals of periods of expectation that were ultimately doomed. This was a treatment that was seemingly programmed to end badly.

The categorization of failure along a time axis does allow for some differences in terms of bad starts, bad processes, and bad endings, but it also highlights the need for more specific causes of failed cases. We turn to this avenue of inquiry in Chapters 6, 7, and 8 and begin in Chapter 9 with an introduction about choosing a particular form of treatment that may not be the best choice.

9

On Losing One's Patience

It is difficult to gather information from the psychoanalytic or psychotherapeutic literature about the failure to retain patients. Although there are many case reports of trying or difficult patients, it is not a commonplace to report on one's failure to keep a patient in treatment. This failure encompasses those patients who leave analysis or psychotherapy quite early in the treatment as well as those who insist upon a premature termination. We shall discuss exceptions to this group later. It would be challenging to deny that the condition or phenomenon of patients successfully completing treatment is, for the most part, considered to be a virtue, whereas the loss of a patient falls into a category somewhat akin to a mistake or a failure. Such a failure quickly becomes attributed to personal irresponsibility on the part of the analyst or therapist, inasmuch as losing a patient is, at least by some definitions, an act of neglect.

In contrast to the lack of detailed clinical material on patient loss, there seems to be much anecdotal discussion in private conversations about patients who quit precipitously, those who never seemed to fully commit to treatment, or those who just do not seem to match well (Kantrowitz, 1995).

In the psychiatric literature, we read of patients who drop out of clinical trials, but this sort of report is ordinarily confined to the trial being too onerous and/or the side effects of medication being too unacceptable. In psychoanalysis or psychotherapy, there is usually an explanation that is expected for dropouts. These explanations can be considered along a timeline with those that occur at the onset of treatment usually (but not always) being attributed to a particular sort of patient pathology, whereas the responsibility for those that occur after a considerable time in therapy or analysis is attributed to the therapist or analyst. The word *blame* is appropriate because of the built-in moral opprobrium often attached to losing a patient.

One can organize the consideration of treatment failures along a timeline. The earliest falls under the category of the therapeutic alliance, followed by those said to occur because of transference–countertransference difficulties. Lastly, there are those that reflect unsuccessful terminations. Although there is a certain neatness to this temporal organization, there can be no doubt that an indeterminate number of treatment failures seem to make no sense. They are inexplicable yet still make the claim that something either was done wrong or else failed to be done right. Losing a patient is ever an error.

THE THERAPEUTIC ALLIANCE

An excellent review of the concept of the therapeutic alliance is presented in a book edited by Levy in which a number of distinguished analysts discuss the concept (Levy, 2000). When Freud referred to the unobjectionable part of the transference, he is said to have meant a positive feature that allows the analysis to progress in spite of its difficulties (Abend, 2000, p. 10). As these discussants dissect the meaning and value of the therapeutic or working alliance, they range from embracing the concept to dismissing it. Renik (2000, p. 96) told us that he feels it has no immediate practical value, and that he is not very much interested in the concept. Greenson (1978) and Zetzel (1966) have written about it with emphasis on its necessity to move an analysis, and they distinguish it from the transference. Brenner (1979) felt that the distinction "is a specious one and that its consequences for analytic practice are, generally speaking, undesirable" (p. 155). The overall conclusion of a more recent paper by Neutzel, Larsen, and Prizmer (2007) is that the therapeutic alliance is the strongest predictor of improvement in patient-reported general adjustment. Much of the argument about the value and worth of the concept is a tug of war over the alliance as distinct from the transference, as claimed by Zetzel and Greenson, or as essentially a product of early maternal transference phenomena (Freedman, 1969).

There seems no easy way to comprehend what factor or factors allow a treatment to succeed unless we introduce some concept that reflects the capacity to progress. Is it safe to assume that the absence of the factor is responsible for failure in treatment? Do we lose patients because of this ingredient, whether or not it reflects an early maternal transference, whether or not it comes about because the therapist gratifies the patient, and whether or not it embodies elements of reality in the therapeutic relationship that are not strong enough to sustain the relationship?

Amidst the very detailed and even labored debate over the existence and origin of the therapeutic alliance, one is led to an unavoidable conclusion that there are factors that allow and aid treatment and there are those that prevent or impede it. The latter have been said by some to merely be the absence of the former (Adler, 2000, p. 76) or perhaps its "fragility" (p. 77). The assumption that underscores these positions is one that claims that healthy patients have what it takes to enable treatment, whereas the sicker, called *borderline* or *narcissistic*, are lacking enough of the necessary stuff. This assumption leads to the logical conclusion that the less disturbed patient should surely be able to form a therapeutic alliance, and if treatment fails it is clearly the fault of the therapist. If, on the other hand, the treatment is successful, then the minimum requirement is the establishment of a good working alliance. Failure comes from patient pathology and analyst or therapist incompetence. Success is a result of healthier patients coupled with therapist expertise.

And yet there seem to be exceptions. At times, a good match in a neurotic patient seen by a competent therapist seems to go nowhere. At times, a poor match in a borderline patient with an inexpert therapist works out well. Are these exceptions to the rule, or is there simply no rule to guide us? We do know of extremely disturbed patients who stay in analysis or therapy and benefit greatly from it as well as those less disturbed patients who get nowhere. The familiar tenet that some patients are simply too ill to be analyzed often extends itself to patients too ill for psychotherapy. Although analyzability is a concept containing a host of requirements, treatability is a looser term filled with qualifying phrases such as *wanting to get better* and *likability*.

Any diagnostic evaluation of a failed analysis or therapy might conclude that there was a bad match, a fragile or broken therapeutic alliance, a resistance that was not adequately interpreted, a countertransference that was allowed unwarranted expression, or a number of other conjectures. Most of these are in the nature of postmortem diagnoses, and only a few are predicted outcomes.

In the majority of case reports, the clinical presentation is one of a patient being evaluated to conform to a specific plan of treatment. We do not read of any significant change in course such as one might imagine if a self psychologist moved to a "mainstream or classical" stance, or if an interpersonalist decided that a Lacanian approach would be more effective. Rather, we have learned to expect a dogged persistence in both attitude and interpretation. It is a rare analyst who can either practice or refer patients for cognitive-behavioral therapy. Yet in a very telling footnote, Abend (2000) did seem to adequately reflect the current state of affairs. He said that analysts who advocate one or another of the approaches of emerging schools of psychoanalysis may have different viewpoints than his, which is confined to "mainstream or traditional psychoanalytic thought" (pp. 11–12). We do what we do and explain both success and failure on the basis of the theoretical approach that is most congenial to us. Perhaps that is a mistake or, at least, a warning sign.

CASE EXAMPLE

Kenneth came for analysis because of a general aimlessness in life. He had graduated from a prominent university but without any clear goals or career path in mind. He had been referred by his mother, who was concerned about his seeming depression, and she had encouraged him to seek treatment. The arrangements for analysis went smoothly, and the initial hours appeared to presage a promising course of treatment. The content of those initial hours, aside from the history, consisted of report after report of an intrusive and interfering father. His father called me. His father read Kenneth's mail on his computer. He tried to overhear his phone conversations. He examined (or so Kenneth thought) his son's bedroom. I thought to myself and interpreted how such activities might upset Kenneth. Soon, Kenneth began to miss appointments. He was quite casual about these misses, and no amount of discussion in the treatment seemed to elicit any concern, and certainly not any plausible explanation. I found myself making interpretation after interpretation to both explain his absences and entice my patient to resume regular attendance. There is no doubt in my mind that my interpretations ranged from the silly to the senseless with an occasional sensible one. All to no avail. Kenneth stopped coming. His father called to tell me how disappointed he was in me. I had lost a patient.

Without a doubt, many readers of the clinical vignette may feel that there is not clinical material to warrant any significant conclusions as to the reason(s) for my failure. According to one school of thought, the therapeutic or working alliance had not been sufficiently established, and so a basic unobjectionable feeling of trust and hope was missing. According to another way of thinking, the patient had indeed established some sort of father transference to an intrusive and meddling analyst and so quickly departed from this form of a relationship. I'm sure a number of other failings could be elicited ranging from my lack of real empathy to my inability to reveal my own feelings to my patient. The underlying theme to these and other possible commentaries is that what happened need not have happened. Someone else would have or could have done a better job. Of this there can be no doubt.

I thought that I had been conducting a "mainstream" psychoanalysis, that a therapeutic alliance had been established, and that I could expect the expectable. Later, I wondered if perhaps my personal subjectivity had not been exposed and expressed. Perhaps an analyst steeped in a more relational position could have been more successful. All sorts of possible alternative ways of conducting the treatment came to mind. Had the fact that Kenneth had come because of his mother's insistence been left unexplained? Did it mean that it was the mother who desired analysis? I longed for a regular conference that discussed treatment that went bad. I remained in a state of self-criticism.

TRANSFERENCE AND COUNTERTRANSFERENCE FACTORS

Although it is certainly an arguable issue, there is some convenience in considering the establishment of a workable transference neurosis following that of the therapeutic alliance. Without doubt, the middle phase of an analysis is a construction that is made by the analyst inasmuch as the formation of a transference is known to begin at the very onset of an analysis. There is a veritable mountain of opinions about the recognition and handling of the transference, and no doubt there is an equal wealth of ideas about how one may lose a patient because of the mishandling of these issues. Indeed, in one sense all matters concerning the loss of a patient boil down to the management of the transference and countertransference, and there is no way to present these problems outside of particular cases.

Supervision is the touchstone for a critique of psychoanalysis and psychotherapy. Ideally it should be ongoing and endless in one form or another, but often it is turned to primarily in times of crisis. This was the case when Dr. J. came to me to discuss a patient that he had lost. He was surprised when the premature ending of this treatment came about and wanted to talk about the abruptness of this quitting because it was so unpredictable; he felt that he had been mistreated and even betrayed by his patient.

CASE EXAMPLE

Susan had come to see Dr. J. because of her persistent and repetitive unfaithfulness to her husband. It was not that she had fallen in love with another man but rather that she had periodic one-night stands that became doubly difficult to understand because she regularly confessed the misdeeds to her husband.

The history of Susan was presented as follows. Her parents were remembered mostly for her shame about them; they kept a terribly dirty and disorganized home. From a very young age, their local priest, an old family friend, would sexually abuse her on a regular basis while babysitting on the parents' bowling night. When she eventually told her parents, years later, the father responded by recognizing that it was wrong, but was unable to act on the matter for fear of ruining the priest's reputation. The father was physically and verbally abusive to the mother, and to both the son and daughter alike, and had always had affairs, which the mother knew about, and for which she always forgave him. She saw the mother as a vulnerable victim, and her father as a self-centered louse.

She met her husband-to-be when she was struggling with her weight—a problem she managed in the context of an eating disorder. At their first meeting she was infatuated with him, while he was lukewarm toward her until their second meeting, some weeks later, by which time she succeeded in becoming much thinner and, to both her and him, much more attractive. The early phase of the marriage was happy on both sides, until she suspected her husband of an e-mail liaison with another woman. She was convinced by her husband's assurances that he never met with the woman, but not by his assurances that he never wanted to. She then developed a habit of going out with her girlfriends, without her husband, and finding cute guys at nightclubs to flirt with and occasionally to take to bed. Her husband's response was stupidly nonsuspicious, and after she eventually told him of her liaisons, he became infuriatingly forgiving, and frustratingly slow to take action, continuing instead as the chauffeur to her girls' nights out, rather than the chaperone. By the time she came in for treatment, she had relegated her husband to a position of financial provider, although she abused him with her cruel retellings of her drunken escapades with boys. Apart from a mild but fading sense of security from returning home to him, she essentially hated him, and he eventually closed the door on the marriage long after she moved out.

The treatment of Susan was quite interesting and even captivating to Dr. J., and he felt that they could work well together. The impetus for his seeking supervision was the announcement of Susan that she was being forced to quit treatment because of finances. Dr. J. and Susan had arranged for her to e-mail him if she was forced to fail an appointment, and just before her announcement of termination she had failed an appointment and had neglected to inform Dr. J. by way of e-mail. He brought this up to her, and she explained that she did not have a computer at home but only at work and so she could not have informed him of her planned cancellation. Dr. J. knew instantly that she was lying because she had earlier written from her home computer. He felt confused and flustered. Should he confront her with this lie? Did she really not have the finances to continue? Dr. J. realized that he had somehow become a stand-in for the cuckolded husband and soon after sought supervision because he had read about the vertical split and narcissistic behavioral disorders from my writings (Goldberg, 1999) and felt that this case was a prime example.

The difference in the reactions of Dr. J. and myself was clear: He felt that he was simply uninformed, whereas I felt in the case of Kenneth that I had done something wrong. He thought that he knew where to turn inasmuch as he attributed his patient loss to an educational deficit, whereas I attributed mine more to a personal dilemma. Now admittedly one could ascribe a countertransference problem to both of these incidents, inasmuch as they both were initiated by a transference reaction elicited from the patient. Dr. J. was quite fortunate to realize and recognize his deficit and so sought remedial help. Although any reader might know how I may have or should have done the same, I was not so fortunate. Dr. J. sought out a supervisor whom he felt had a clear theory as to the nature of the problem as well as the remedy, whereas I had no such clarity of direction. More to the point, Dr. J. was free enough to commit to a new agenda, but I was perhaps too fixed in my position.

WISHING TO LOSE A PATIENT

A category of patients that undoubtedly exists but is rarely discussed is one that falls under the negative connotation introduced in Chapter 7 and consists of patients we want to be rid of. I can at this time only present a case in which the wish was conscious, but it is certainly true that such a wish may mainly be operant unconsciously.

CASE EXAMPLE

Clark was a young man who came for treatment for a variety of symptoms ranging from compulsively checking to see if he had locked his door to hypochondriacal preoccupation with the state of his health. I saw Clark for several years in psychotherapy as he recounted a troubled past with divorced parents, a sister who had died of a drug overdose, a mother who was herself in treatment and urged Clark to get me to prescribe one drug after another, and a rather distant father. The treatment of Clark was, for the most part, successful, and he managed to graduate from law school and obtain steady work. There was no doubt on my part that Clark was a difficult patient, and I regularly sensed my inner dismay as the time for his appointment(s) neared.

Clark stopped—or, more appropriately, interrupted—his treatment on several occasions only to return at times of crisis. The last one centered on his involvement with a young woman and his wish to get engaged to her, a wish that was unlikely to be satisfied because of the fights and disagreements that broke out with her. As I listened to the content of his latest return, I felt that Clark needed more than the therapy that I had been offering, and that I needed to rid myself of Clark. I suggested that Clark go into psychoanalysis and that he do so with someone else. I explained at length the difference between therapy and analysis and urged that he do the latter.

My referral of Clark to someone else was accompanied by a significant sense of relief. I honestly felt that my advice was sound, although my motives were suspect. Clark was puzzled by my position and left with something short of an agreement to follow my directions. I later learned that he went into therapy with someone else. I felt bad about that but glad that he no longer made me dread his presence. My own transference allowed me to lose a patient. However, I was also committed to a particular theory that insisted on my personal self-analysis to handle my feelings about a patient. Another theory (Mitchell, 1995) might have me share my feelings with the patient inasmuch as we had co-constructed the therapeutic situation. Once again, one can see how we remain ever faithful to the way our theory insists things should be.

PREMATURE TERMINATION AND
EVER-RECEDING TERMINATION

In what seems like a mild contradiction to the main thrust of this chapter, the problem of termination and loss is twofold: Some patients quit treatment rather than endure the difficulties of the termination phase, whereas some never are allowed to quit for the same reason. The latter is often an illustration of a therapist or analyst not wanting to endure the loss of a patient. Although we regularly see a premature termination as "a flight into health," we are reluctant to see "permanent patients" as reflecting the vulnerability of analysts or therapists to a loss. This is the exception to the usual concept of loss noted earlier.

CASE EXAMPLE

Ms. C. was a middle-aged woman referred to me with the description "the most severe case of hypochondriasis I have ever seen." She was referred by her first analyst, who had terminated her analysis when he retired, but the termination did not appear successful inasmuch as Mrs. C. developed severe anxiety and asked for a referral. Another analysis was entered into and seemed successful, and after several years another termination was suggested. Once again, Mrs. C. developed severe anxiety and asked to continue her treatment albeit at a much reduced frequency. Once an arrangement was made that Mrs. C. be seen weekly for as long as she wished, her anxiety markedly diminished and only seemed to surface during separations that went on for extended periods.

I literally could not lose this patient, and I discovered that many of my colleagues had similar examples of such permanent patients. Were these to be seen as problems in a true resolution of the transference, which they certainly were, or as a subcategory of analysands who perhaps did need a never-ending treatment? Of course, I cannot presently answer that question, but it does highlight what may be the major problem in the conundrum of patient loss (i.e., the differentiation of the treatment from those who are treated). We, at the present time, do not possess a clear classification of psychological disorders that would enable us to match treatment and patient. The match that Kantrowitz (1995) wrote about may be relevant not only to patient and therapist but also to treatment and therapist. Perhaps Abend's (2000) allegiance to "mainstream psychoanalysis" is best seen as one form of treatment that works well with one kind of patient, just as Kohut's ideas work well with others. And so the problem that lies behind some patient losses may be just this sort of mismatch.

DISCUSSION

In a very compelling article about the present state of psychoanalysis, at least in the United States, Cooper (2008) concluded that
there are both a number of different schools of thought and an
equal number of authoritarian orthodoxies. Thus, we live in an age
of pluralism along with certainty. Cooper bemoaned the failure of
a true scientific discourse that would allow us to determine what
is really effective and so might resolve what he feels is the present
state of chaos.

At the onset, one needs to differentiate a pluralism that has a
number of different approaches or solutions to the same problem from one that insists upon different approaches to different
problems. For example, a number of different antibiotics may cure
one particular form of infection, whereas different infectious diseases may demand different treatments. Under the first category,
one may aim for and hope for a refinement of competing agents
to determine the single best one. Many scientific disciplines and
many treatment efforts need to pass through a period of growth
and development to achieve this best possible solution. Under
the second category, the need is to determine how to differentiate what may be different forms of pathology as well as different
forms of therapy. Quite often, especially in medicine, we come
across an effective therapy that works well in one illness tried out
on a variety of what seem to be closely allied illnesses. We see this
in cancer treatments that work well in one form of malignancy
and fail completely in others.

The position that Cooper (2008) stated as one that reflects today's
analysis seems to suggest a plethora of orthodox approaches that
resist refinement because they do not talk to one another. He did
not much emphasize the possibility that some treatments do well
with one approach and some with another, although he did consider that point in his reference to Kohut. However, his principle
lament was that of each school being so closed to discourse with

other schools that it allows for no opportunity for such needed refinement. Summers (2008) echoed this unfortunate state and made the claim that dialogue will aid in the cure. There can be no doubt of the reality of these authoritarian orthodoxies or of their self-proclaimed assurances to have the right answers. However, it may well be the case that one's effectiveness as an analyst or therapist depends upon and needs a sense of conviction that one is indeed doing what is right along with the feeling that others are merely misguided. If that is true, then the answer to Cooper's dilemma will not come from increased discourse. We well know from discussions between believers in different religions that they rarely lead to either person abandoning one set of beliefs for another. We may become more tolerant, but we hardly ever abandon our sense of certainty. This sense of certainty is surely the "orthodoxy" that Cooper condemned. We may be misguided more to application than to belief. One possibility that is often entertained but, sadly, never truly studied is that some theories appeal to certain personalities, and some to others. Thus, behind the Kantrowitz (1995) match of style and character there may lurk a commitment to a certain form of conduct in practice. If, for instance, one reads the very compelling article by Mari Ruti (2008) that is designed according to the author to "explain to a non-Lacanian audience the broad philosophical foundations of Lacanian theory" (p. 483), it may seem evident that to practice in the manner of a Lacanian analyst would seem to require a particular philosophical outlook. In a very telling footnote, Ruti (2008) distinguished the deconstructive form of analysis that would be Lacanian from the restorative form that "allows one to rewrite one's past along affirmative lines" (p. 494). Without delving too deeply into the differences between a Lacanian analysis and (say) an ego psychologist, one can easily see the appeal of the one or the other. Interestingly, most (but not all) of the references in the Ruti article that support Lacan are from nonclinicians.

The problem of patient loss is of course more complex than what is suggested here because of the myriad external factors ranging from financial to geographical difficulties. Patients move and encounter money problems. They marry and get sick and quit treatment accordingly. But if we put to the side all of these real environmental factors, then it seems quite likely that the simple fact is that some treatments work with some patients, and some with others, and most analysts and therapists are not able to shift gears when a change is needed. Today's pluralism reflects the insularity of schools of theory and technique that does not allow for analysts or therapists to become expert in alternative efforts. At one time, a prominent analytic training program that taught "classical psychoanalysis" prided itself on offering a course with the title Deviant Schools of Psychoanalysis. At best, the analytic institute and psychotherapy training programs that strive to present these alternative techniques are quite unable to determine the matching of patient pathology with preferable treatment. Rather, we often do match patient and therapist. But these matches, as admirable as the effort may be, cannot go beyond personality to (say) help an interpersonal therapist decide that a classical or a Lacanian analysis is called for in a particular patient. We do what we do, and we regularly and sometimes persistently keep on doing it. Sometimes it works, and sometimes we lose patients.

Starting with the unavoidable premise that we are not all successful in analyzing and treating every patient, we might all profit from copying the conferences, which go on with varying titles in all medical schools, that discuss treatment failures. The two lines of discussion that develop in these conferences are either those devoted to contributions that say what might have been done to change a failure to a success or those that conclude that nothing more or different could have been done. Each form of inquiry can be profitable. However, one profits only if one can both entertain a change and also have the competence to do so. Unfortunately, most of us employ a single lens of theory and technique and cannot imagine or believe in dispensing with it and employing another. This allegiance to doing what we do is not to be condemned, because it may well be responsible for our effectiveness. Stubbornness is not uncommon in our field, and it may well be necessary and even admirable.

There are cases that we seem unable to lose, and there are those that everyone might lose. However, the bulk of cases that we lose may not have been lost with another approach, not merely another analyst or therapist but also another set of ideas. The combination of orthodoxy and the possible efficacy of this trait leads to an impasse that seems capable of resolution only if we were someday to evolve to a single and optimal mode of treatment. Today's pluralism defies that likelihood. We do indeed do things differently, and we are not growing more alike. Perhaps the best hope for the future is working toward a better determination of what works best for particular patients no matter what we do and do best.

Different patients may require more than a match of personalities between patient and therapist. The requirement goes beyond such superficial, although quite important, factors to a more basic one (i.e., of theory). Certain patients may do well with "mainstream psychoanalysis," others with interpersonal therapy, others with CBT, others with self psychology, and so on. Just as we are beginning to learn that some antidepressant medications work with some patients and not with others, and there is no way to predetermine the efficacy of one medication over another, so the same may be true of forms of treatment based upon psychological approaches. It is simply not true that an expert practitioner steeped in one theoretical approach can apply his or her methodology to all patients, yet we continue to compare approaches to a single patient and argue over which is best. We often guess as to the ideal referral of a patient, but we have not lifted such guesses to the level of a scientific explanation. We lose patients not only because of incompetence or mere bad luck, but also because of our being locked into what we take to be universal truths.

10
Analyzability and Failure

A common and almost universally accepted tool of evaluation for psychoanalysis is that of analyzability. The categories that are used to assess the capacity to undergo and so to profit from psychoanalysis are also fairly well agreed upon (Paolino, 1981). They include psychological mindedness as a leading asset. This includes (a) the capacity to perceive the relationship between thoughts, feelings, and action; (b) the capacity and desire to learn the meanings and causes of experience and behavior; and (c) the capacity to direct thinking toward one's own psychic life. Other desirable assets include the desire for less psychic pain, the capacity to experience feelings within the session, a positive attitude toward analysis from one's family and friends, the lack of an overwhelming present-day crisis, the capacity to not act out, the capacity to develop and maintain a therapeutic relationship, and a good fit between patient and analyst. A frequently added ingredient is that of a need for psychoanalysis; although it may be true that all of the requirements for analyzability are subjective ones, this last is perhaps the most subjective of them all: It is based on a cost–benefit analysis and really concerns whether one should be analyzed rather than if one can be analyzed.

In all branches of medicine, and perhaps in the entire world devoted to developing solutions for problems, the ordinary sequence of such efforts at solutions has been that of the diagnosis followed, where possible, by the treatment. At times, a treatment becomes so significant and even glamorized that it seems to dominate or even obviate the diagnosis; this, perhaps unfortunately, has been true in the practice of psychoanalysis. Indeed, a recent article entitled "Why We Recommend Analytic Treatment for Some Patients and Not for Others" (Caligor et al., 2009) confronts this inversion of the sequence head on and concludes that all patients should enter analysis in order to determine whether "patient based moderators of analytic treatment can be identified" (p. 694). Lacking such moderators, it would seem that there are no clear guidelines, save possibly for extreme cases, that allow one to pick and choose among alternative treatments and so to recommend psychoanalysis as especially indicated for some patients. Thus, everyone gets the treatment on the road to determine just who may benefit from it.

As with many seemingly established tenets in psychoanalysis, it may be worthwhile to consider if the assumptions about analyzability are valid. It may be the case that these "taken-for-granted" points conceal fantasies that need to see the light of day. Many so-called rescue fantasies are accompanied by grandiose aspects with fundamentally unrealistic narcissistic components. Perhaps analyzability need have no guarantee of a positive result "as long as no errors are made," inasmuch as this may place the analysis of countertransference in an unwarranted pivotal position. An examination of failed cases may allow us to have a more reasonable set of expectations about analysis. It is often quite difficult to accept the concept of either an untreatable or, perhaps better said, an unchangeable patient. It may be more comfortable and less narcissistically injurious to embrace error rather than impotence.

It should not be surprising that uncertainty about a tight connection between diagnosis and treatment might well result in misfits that fail to yield positive results. With an emphasis placed on analyzability (i.e., the capacity to be analyzed) as the most important feature in recommending analysis, we might well end up with patients being analyzed, perhaps even successfully analyzed, and yet not being much helped. The crucial word in the previous sentence is *successfully*, and so one presumes that that means symptom relief and whatever else one attributes to "success." Of course, there is an old surgical joke that ends with "the operation was a success, but the patient died." In psychoanalysis, we may fall back on the insistence that all analysis promises to do is to foster understanding; everything else such as symptom relief is but a byproduct. More often than not, we collapse analyzability into success and conclude that failures in analysis really mean that the patient was not analyzable. We never can contemplate a well-analyzed patient remaining unchanged, nor do we often reckon with a patient who indeed could be analyzed not being advised to do so, with considerations of time and money being put aside (i.e., if you can, you should).

Patients do enter into psychoanalytic treatment with a range of goals from understanding themselves, to the relief of particular symptoms, up to and including vague goals such as feeling genuinely fulfilled or specific ones such as getting married or divorced. At times, it may be the case that a specific goal in an analyzable person is considered able to be achieved without an analysis (and this will later be considered under the separate category of treatability), but it is probably true that for those practicing psychoanalysis, analyzability rules the day.

If we were to separate analyzability from its goals (i.e., consider a certain group of analyzable patients with problems not likely to be helped by analysis) along with a group of problems that could clearly be best helped by procedures other than analysis, we might be better able to ascertain just when we consider an analysis to be a failure. Thus, we might judge a case to be a failure where analysis was undertaken yet definitely not indicated in spite of the patient's analyzability, along with a case where analysis might have helped if only the patient were analyzable. These conditions seem never or perhaps rarely to happen as long as analyzability is the determining factor in recommending analysis. It seems that we often do not know when to recommend analysis.

Psychoanalysis may well exemplify a problem that exists throughout all of psychiatry—the determination of what treatment should be offered for what disorder. The person who offers the treatment may not have a full armamentarium of treatments to offer and so does whatever he or she is best at.

CLINICAL EXAMPLE

A case presented in a seminar on failed cases seemed to represent an analysis that was not to be faulted in its conduct, yet resulted in an unchanged patient. The case will not be presented, inasmuch as there is a high probability that someone would find some fault in the conduct of the analysis; there is regularly a relentless search for mistakes in failed cases. However, for the most part every point that was raised in the ensuing discussion in the seminar seemed to have been considered. The major issues were discussed. There seemed to be a good working alliance, an interpretable transference, and a careful consideration of any countertransference issues. To be sure, this was a troubled soul who had had several courses of psychotherapy to no avail. Some listeners insisted that the patient had been helped in spite of the parallel conviction of patient and analyst that this was simply untrue. Point after point that was raised to demonstrate the patient's improvement was countered by a reminder that all of this was true before the patient began the analysis. Once this point was firmly established, there was a brief move to insist that the patient would have been much worse if he had not been in analysis. Thus, the move from change to maintaining the status quo became the vehicle of support for analysis.

After the consideration of what seemed to be a failed analysis, one may conclude that this particular patient should not have been taken into analysis or that the analysis was poorly or improperly conducted. The first conclusion is usually, but not always, equated with analyzability. The second, that of incompetence, is the most common preoccupation of supervision or case discussions. A third option of mere misapplication is not considered. However, there are a number of variations of psychoanalysis that have been developed over the years that claim to be more effective than the classical or orthodox form of psychoanalysis and are put forth as being representative of analysis. Not surprisingly, such deviations from classical analysis are perceived by some as truly being deviant and so tossed into the category of mere psychotherapy. Thus failure is rescued in a new form; it would not be a failed case if a different approach had been pursued. Perhaps the classical analyst would say the failure merely reflected a case that was not analyzable and again collapse the two categories, whereas the proponent of alternate approaches would expand the category of analysis and propose a different process that many might insist is not really analysis. Analyzability and inevitable improvement of whatever sort go hand in hand for some.

TREATABILITY

No doubt a combination of courage, creativity, and perseverance has led to a variety of alterations and modifications in psychoanalysis. Self psychology, relational analysis, and interpersonal and intersubjective analysis are some examples of treatments that are derived from psychoanalysis and are championed by their proponents as more or less universally applicable and effective. There are probably as many voices of dissent as to the worth of these alternative or modified approaches as there are those of support, but one loud voice of dissent is that these approaches do not qualify as being truly psychoanalytic; they are psychotherapeutic and therefore a somewhat lesser form of activity. Likewise, a staunch proponent of any of these supposed alternate or deviant schools might take the position that theirs was the basic or proper approach and deviations from their position would be a lesser form of treatment. Inasmuch as a majority of these alternate approaches are a result of the widening scope of analysis, the stakes are raised for explaining or rationalizing failure, and inevitably the resultant explanation for failure was bad performance ranging from countertransference problems to sheer incompetence. As more and more patients were considered treatable, there remained less room for a category of mistaken application (i.e., treatment was not advised).

Therefore, patients were placed in separate categories by those separate schools of psychoanalysis. However, the stance that insists that once one was deemed as properly able to be analyzed by such placement, then change or improvement would naturally follow, did not vary.

To move from a consideration of psychoanalysis for a patient to that of psychotherapy requires a somewhat treacherous path. The journey starts with some particular form of evaluation of the psychoanalysis that is recommended. Thus, a statement (that takes many shapes) that this patient could not benefit from a classical approach but needed (say) an intersubjective analysis would begin the assignment. That may or may not be followed by considerations of gender, the personality of the analyst, the frequency of visits, and other parameters. In its most simplified form, no case is a failure unless it is properly situated, and the only cause for failure is a mistaken placement. It is difficult to generalize about the many different forms of psychoanalysis that are extant from Lacanian to Kleinian to Kohutian and on to the many others that exist. For the most part, the modifications that are enlisted such as (say) frequency do tend to make a clear distinction. Analysis per se becomes somewhat fuzzy, and some schools may resist any such distinction whatsoever. However, for those who clearly differentiate psychoanalysis from psychotherapy, there does appear to be a change in attitude, one that has certain expectations for one and quite different ones for the other.

Cases of psychotherapy from either one or another of these different schools of psychoanalysis or from any type of activity described as psychoanalytic or psychodynamic therapy are usually seen as less constrained in terms of both frequency and the activity of the therapist. Patients may be seen once or twice per week, and often the couch is not employed. Behavior that may qualify as a violation of a boundary, although not egregious but still unacceptable, is allowed or even encouraged. Yet failure is not unknown. However, when a failed case was presented to our conference as a failure in psychotherapy, a different response was regularly elicited.

One presentation of a treatment failure was uniformly initially endorsed by those listening as suitable for treatment. The patient was seen two times a week, sitting up, with regular attendance and with little evidence of any countertransference problems. The case had been one that was initially considered for psychoanalysis, but it had been changed to psychotherapy because the patient was felt to be unanalyzable. Once again, this became the determining feature in the assignment of treatment.

As the presentation of the case (and later noted for many such cases) continued, and as it became clearer that the psychotherapy was not being effective, the members of the seminar rarely criticized the presenting therapist or offered many suggestions as to what might have been done. What might possibly be termed the *atmosphere* in the conference room seemed different in a case of psychotherapy that failed than in one of psychoanalysis that delivered little or no improvement. There remained the usual ideas and "hope" that the patient had really done better, or that the patient might have been worse off if not for the treatment, but rarely was there a sharp criticism for the therapist's failure. The issue of responsibility or blame appeared to shift from therapist to patient. The probability that any given patient might be characterized as "untreatable" was given greater voice than in the discussions of patients undergoing psychoanalysis. Perhaps the overall impression of the discussion was a lack of clear rules as to what comprised treatability. In contrast to analyzability, there seemed to exist a lack of standards as to the technique of the therapist that allowed both a greater freedom for intervention that might even be thought of as greater creativity.

ASSESSING FAILURE

Analyzability stands in sharp contrast to treatability by means other than psychoanalysis. If one fulfills the criteria from whatever school of analysis that is proposed, the working assumption is one of ultimate success. Failure results from mistakes in the process. Treatability by psychotherapy is different in that it allows for a properly pursued process that is ineffective no matter how well it is practiced. Failure results from the intractability of the pathology, which in turn is felt to reside in the patient. In the practice of psychoanalysis, the patient may well resist the procedure, but that is anticipated and capable of being mastered. In psychotherapy, patients may just not be able to prosper from the process. The responsibility for a failure is more or less shared by the intractability of the pathology, which is felt to be due to something in the patient, and the limitations of the therapeutic process. The portion of responsibility assigned to the patient varies according to the particular theory of therapy. Much of this is turned on its head when one encounters how general psychiatry deals with treatment failure.

TREATMENT RESISTANCE

The very idea of *treatment resistance* in general psychiatry probably begins with a linguistic challenge inasmuch as one is never exactly certain as to just who or what is doing the resisting. It seems the phrase is used when any of the treatment modalities of general psychiatry outside of psychodynamic psychotherapy fail to work. It is not the patient who is responsible but rather the disease that is resisting the treatment. The patient is never at fault, because he or she is merely the carrier of the affliction. The treatment, usually medication, works sometimes and fails at other times, but other than when a change in dosage is called for it is hardly at fault. *Treatment resistance* satisfies all the requirements for a euphemism of *failure*. The underlying implicit assumption is that of an effective treatment that is being prevented from dealing with an illness because of some unseen factors. We referred to a recent article in Chapter 4 (Brent et al., 2009) that used the phrase with an acronym of TORDIA (treatment of resistant depression in adolescence) to focus on resistance to medication but actually considered other treatment (save that of psychodynamic psychotherapy in the patient population that was studied). Of course, this cohort of patients was in no way resisting treatment, but rather was exhibiting the ineffectiveness of a particular group of medications. Perhaps the proper consideration of this lack of efficacy would be to outline the limitations of the treatment rather than the resistance of the patient with his or her malady.

SITUATING RESPONSIBILITY

The usual reaction to the failure of any particular treatment to effect a positive change in a patient is to situate the responsibility or blame for the failure. In medicine, the postmortem meetings on treatment failures usually consist of a discussion about alternative efforts in treatment, but they rarely single out anyone to bear the responsibility for what is often felt to be an inevitable result. Untreatability is a common feature in many medical scenarios. Something akin to this is also common in general psychiatry, which may offer a host of treatments in an effort to settle on something that works. As we move toward psychodynamic psychotherapy, the therapist becomes prominent as the crucial variable in determining the success or failure of a given treatment in a given patient, but there is room for avoiding responsibility or blame by making the claim that a patient is simply untreatable. This last resort in avoiding responsibility is closed to analysts who have used analyzability as a form of promissory note for improvement. Indeed, there seems to be little or no room for untreatability once analyzability has been allowed in to determine what is a proper course of treatment for a patient. Once placed in the position of responsibility, analysts are able to be seen as both vulnerable and grandiose. They have locked themselves into a rigid bind that insists that treatment failure is the result of a mistake rather than inevitability. We would do well to reexamine the narcissistic fantasy of rescue that underlies the conviction that an analyzable person should necessarily be helped unless someone does something wrong.

DISCUSSION

If one compares the recommendation of Caligor et al. (2009), who wrote of choosing patients for psychoanalysis by suggesting that everyone should enter analysis in order to eventually identify "patient-based moderators," with the very similar actions of the psychiatrists who place all suicidal patients on selective serotonin reuptake inhibitors (SSRIs) in order to identify treatment resistance, we seem to encounter identical efforts of something akin to rolling the dice and hoping to score. It is certainly faster and cheaper to prescribe an SSRI than to start an analysis, but at least compared to psychotherapy there is no evidence whatsoever that medication is more effective (Shedler, 2010). Interestingly, no one is ever labeled as *analysis resistant* or *psychotherapy resistant*, although "resistance" is considered a common feature in all efforts at psychotherapy. *Treatment resistance* is a blanket term to cover all those modalities of treatment, including cognitive-behavioral therapy (CBT) but excluding psychodynamic psychotherapy, that fail to deliver a change for the better.

A simplified way of categorizing patients who fail to improve in one form of treatment would range from failed analysis to failed dynamic psychotherapy to failed CBT to failed medication. Each of these categories has its own parameters for success or failure, but it seems to be true that they all tend to be evaluated within one category. That is to say that if one fails psychoanalysis, he or she then is free to try something else and so on with the other forms of treatment. Most analysts do not medicate. Most psychopharmacologists do not analyze. And perhaps each group would claim that that is the way things should be. No doubt there are mixed groups, and this is perhaps prominent in those psychotherapists who also medicate as well as those psychopharmacologists who practice psychotherapy. The lack of sufficient training in another category does not allow for much competence in most mixed categories, and one cannot presently predict if these separate forms of treatment will continue to grow further apart. Therefore, after a failed analysis, the freedom to go elsewhere usually means little more than resignation without redirection. This is strikingly similar to the situation of treatment-resistant psychiatric patients who have exhausted the list of medications.

Imagine, if you will, a psychiatrist or any mental health professional trained in psychoanalysis, CBT, various schools of analytic psychotherapy, and psychopharmacology. This super psychiatrist (we will call him) evaluates all psychiatric patients in order to assign them to the one mode of treatment that has the highest probability of success. He takes all socioeconomic factors into account as well. The objectivity ascribed to this imaginary figure derives from his not being wedded to one or another treatment modality, along with a firm belief that all treatments are capable of success with the right patient fit as well as the corollary belief that some patients may improve with a number of different therapies. Two forms of failure may result. The first is that of misassignment—the patient should have been analyzed but was medicated. As an aside, one may consider the popularity of a biopsychosocial perspective on all psychological difficulties (Ghaemi, 2010). This orientation insists that all manner of issues needs to be considered, and so ideally everything matters for everyone. Therefore, one may conclude that every failure to improve results from a lack of some sort. Everything from genetics to not offering CBT can be held responsible. Misassignment is close to a universal blame. The second form of failure is a variation on incompetence and ranges from prescribing the wrong drug to one or another form of countertransference difficulty. The assumption here is that the right approach was chosen, but the application failed. Is there a place for a third category, something akin to treatment resistance? In this group, the correct treatment was correctly performed yet was a failure. That very question reveals the fundamental flaw that may exist in all of psychiatry but especially in psychoanalysis with all of its tributaries. We have a form of therapy that may be employed for some persons but not for others, and that may be effective for some of the people for which it is employed and not for others, and so sadly may be a waste of time and money not only because of incompetence but also because of misapplication.

Inasmuch as the psychoanalyst and/or the psychotherapist is the tool of the treatment, one cannot easily generalize about the success or failure of analysis. Each individual analyst serves as a criterion of his or her own success. Analyzability can be considered for a wide population of patients, but the individual application of analysis has no standard for success or failure. Thus, each analysis may be compared to the use of a medication that differs from a similar set of medications. We now know that even amongst SSRIs, some work for some patients and not for others. Possibly the comparison of efficacy over large enough populations can minimize these differences. Short of that, each analyst or therapist has his or her own percentage of successes, and the field as a whole is an average of good and bad therapeutic efforts. However, there does seem to be a difference between analysis and dynamic psychotherapy. The former has a rather established evaluation process that determines analyzability, and thus the variability in success results from differences in analysts and their personal application of the procedure. The latter is less well defined, with treatability seen as a more diffuse category with uncertain boundaries resulting in a variable success rate that may have little to do with the competence of the treater and the correct application of the procedure. Society has given psychiatry a domain of relevance; we are directed to alter what the social network sees as abnormal. The same is true of psychoanalysis and psychotherapy. The boundaries of these domains are vague and have been formed by the needs and values of our social network rather than by the efficacy of our therapeutic work. We would do well to rethink why and when and for what we do what we do.

11

How Does Analysis Fail?

Any therapeutic endeavor has to pass through a series of trials and errors before it is shown to be effective. It likewise has to endure a number of failures before it can be seen to have a particular range of applicability. When Freud introduced psychoanalysis to the world, it was specifically designed to treat the psychoneuroses, and the theoretical background for this limited area of effectiveness was based upon an explanation of the nature of neurotic psychopathology along with an explanation of just how psychoanalysis corrected or relieved this sort of disorder. Over the years, the technique of psychoanalysis expanded (Wallerstein, 1986), and it was felt to be applicable to a wide variety of psychological maladies ranging from psychoses (Ogden, 1982), to borderline pathology (Kernberg, 1975), to narcissistic disorders (Kohut, 1971) to behavior disorders (Goldberg, 2000), and especially (and perhaps unwisely) to anyone and everyone who might possibly benefit from it. Some of the recommended uses did involve a modification of the technique (Kohut, 1971), but many insisted upon a technique that was felt to be classical and unchangeable. The modifications that were suggested were not universally accepted, and so different schools backed by different theoretical approaches came into existence. Not surprisingly, a failure in one technical approach could readily be attributed to a lack of flexibility in trying one or another technical modification.

Rather than a free exchange and sharing of both effectiveness and limitations, there has developed a more deliberate differentiation between so-called schools of psychoanalysis. Therefore, any therapeutic failure should be judged both as occurring within one system of thought and also in comparison with other schools; the question as to whether it would also be considered a failure with a different approach must be part of the inquiry. That is not usually the way most failures are considered. However, such a more global examination is probably a minimum requirement when we ask what might have been done to make a failure into a success. This is a move that focuses less on blame and mistakes and more on the question of what else might have been done.

HAPPENSTANCE

Because the usual practice of psychoanalysis takes an extended period of time, it is more than likely that many events, both expected and untoward, may occur during this time period. Some of these events may be seen as positive, and some as negative, but it is highly probable that they will affect the progress of the treatment. No doubt, many such positive events such as marriage, job promotion, or a move to a different city may significantly alter the treatment and may even be felt to be an indication of the value of the treatment. However, other events such as sickness, job loss, or a move to a different city can negatively affect the treatment and can even be said to contribute to a therapeutic failure. Not all such events are dramatic; some are quite subtle while having significant effects. All in all, it is difficult to determine success or failure in *dynamic systems*, which by definition are those that are necessarily unstable and changing.

A study of failed cases must consider the initial pathology, the correct or incorrect choice of a particular treatment modality to that pathology, the correct or incorrect practice of the chosen treatment modality, and the myriad of possible interfering or supporting external factors that may impinge upon the treatment.

Psychoanalysis, like so many therapeutic endeavors, is always hitting a moving target and does not have the luxury of a fixed application on a fixed disorder.

THE DEFINITION

The concept of failure implies some form of a normative scale that is used to evaluate and position every patient. Such a scale derives from a theory of the attainment of optimum or desirable health, and each and every theory is bolstered by a corresponding separate aspect of the theory, one that relies on the process resulting in reaching a set goal. The process is one of normal development if one considers a patient in one perspective, or else is one of therapeutic action if seen from another perspective. We aim to move patients from one point to another based upon a normative scale that guides our thinking.

Analytic theories are not of one piece. Some aim to make the unconscious conscious, some strive for symptom relief, some attempt to bolster a fragile self or to strengthen a weak ego, some aim to form meaningful relationships, and even some try to do all or none of the above. A normative plan may be openly announced or may lurk in the shadows, but change or movement has to have a sign of recognition, and failure is either a lack of change or a move away from the desired path. Because of the diversity of theories and the corresponding likely diversity of normative scales, improvement and failure may well mean one thing for some treatments and quite a different one for others. When anyone insists that our goal in analysis is not symptom relief but rather insight, he or she has in mind one's own roadmap for success. No doubt, insight may well coincide with the relief of symptoms, but that was not the normative scale being employed. Thus, the tag of *success* or *failure* conceals a multitude of meanings.

The corollary to a normative scale is that of pathology, and here we find a mixture of a cultural norm plus a subjective or very personal one. When homosexuality was considered to be pathological, there was an obvious disparity between the two ways of evaluation. When it was declared to be normal (with all the ensuing exceptions and caveats), there was a collapse of the cultural and personal norms into one. In contrast to this are the many illnesses from depression to schizophrenia that enjoy a universal claim of pathology. Yet we see in psychiatry's struggle with *DSM-V* (American Psychiatric Association, forthcoming) that there is an actual competition among many syndromes from road rage to excessive shopping regarding their earning a rightful place in being labeled as *psychopathological.*

The advantage of the position focusing solely on insight is that it bypasses pathology almost entirely: Everyone with the overall goal of insight can or should be analyzed without much concern about diagnostic categories. There was, of course, a very clear consideration of what was allowed to pass for pathology. That was represented in the categories of analyzability and nonanalyzability, with the latter reserved for those too sick to be helped by analysis. The vagueness of the cardinal carrier of change (i.e., cure) has over time been elaborated on by a number of authors.

Jacques Lacan, although employing a number of idiosyncratic words and phrases, was quite clear as to his idea of cure. Fink (1997) claimed that Lacan insisted that "the goal of analysis, as Lacan conceptualized it in the early 1950s, is to pierce through the imaginary dimension which veils the symbolic and confront the analysand's relations to the Other head on" (p. 35). Later, Fink said that the symbolic dimension is "the only dimension that cures." Symbolic relations are said to be the way people deal with the ideals inculcated in them by their parents and society at large, and so Lacan felt the aim of analysis is to clarify and modify the analysand's symbolic relations.

Again according to Fink (1997), in the later work of Lacan, the goal of analysis is modified so that one is never free of the Other, but rather one reconstitutes oneself. Thus, the goal allows one to obtain satisfaction with the inhibition of desire (Fink, 1997, p. 210). This seems to equate the end of analysis with a state of acceptance or resignation, such as is said to be articulated by Sándor Ferenczi.

Heinz Kohut may have brought a bit more clarity to the problem in *How Does Analysis Cure?* (1984) when he explained to us the title of his book and so allowed us to infer that the essence of failure is the result of cure (i.e., structure building) apparently not happening. The essential ingredient in Kohut's concept of cure had to do with the building up of psychic structure, itself a theoretical construction, and the formation of a stable self-structure. To be sure, there is no easy way to measure such achievements, but there is a window that is offered that enables one to assess the presence or absence of such a structure, or perhaps to ultimately quantify psychic structure and so determine a level of change in that entity (Grande et al., 2009). This assessment is different than the insight offered, although each may be a proper barometer of success, and both may occur.

The Boston Change Process Study Group (BCPSG; see Nahum, 2002) seemed to turn the entire process of change and cure on its head. For them, the therapeutic interaction consists of "intention units" that are co-created, represented nonsymbolically, and not necessarily a result of interpretation. The therapeutic interaction informed by developmental "relational" imperatives allows different and equally effective pathways to a final therapeutic destination (BCPSG, 2008). It would appear that various forms of conversation may well lead to someone "getting better" without any particular operant concept. Although explained in retrospect as a developmental achievement, there does seem to be somewhat of a mystery to improvement. There seems less of a mystery about failure, inasmuch as the patient simply does not get better, nor does he or she have an increase or decrease in insight or in psychic structure.

Attachment theory, interpersonal and relational theories, along with a number of other categories of therapeutic interventions that lay claim to being variants of psychoanalysis have different ways of conceptualizing the nature of pathology and cure. For the most part, they do not consider insight and the undoing of repression as the sine qua non of analytic cure, nor do they finesse the whole idea as the Boston Change Process Study Group does, which will be elaborated on in Chapter 11. We seem left with the dilemma that different groups embracing different theories claim that what they do makes people better and/or promotes changes in people and that these changes are desirable. Most of the pathology that these groups focus upon resides in failure of optimal development, and the failure is undone or corrected by the particular therapeutic activity espoused by the group. A dilemma arises from the fact that either a given developmental disturbance can be corrected or cured by a variety of means, or else different developmental disturbances require a specific form of treatment. In the first case, anything works. In the second case, each problem must be matched with one or perhaps more specific therapeutic modalities. Attachment theory comes close to ferreting out a specific developmental problem, but all sorts of treatments are said to be effective for these specific problems. However, all or most theories carve out some failure in development that their therapy best fits. It appears both that anything works and that there are specific treatments for specific failures. Most analytic therapies say that whatever they do substitutes for, makes up for, or alleviates what was not done properly during childhood. However, that cannot possibly be said for the classical stance of interpretation, which surely was not considered to be a necessary ingredient of normal development. Indeed, that does seem to correspond to Gitelson's insistence that analysis need only lead to enhanced understanding, whereas everything else such as symptom relief is best considered a byproduct.

The conclusion that seems to result from the plethora of ways of assessing cure or failure is clearly one dependent on the preliminary assessment of the patient's position on a scale of pathology or health. If one aims to make the unconscious conscious, then everyone who can be analyzed thereby qualifies. If one aims for symptom relief, a new set of criteria applies; so, too, for structure building, the modification of symbolic relations, and so on. Without dismissing the possible conclusion that one may accomplish a successful analysis that satisfies all of the theories and the scales no matter what presuppositions are assumed, the more likely conclusion may be that one form of analytic work may succeed in its own process while not at all fulfilling the requirements of a different form. It is no wonder that our theories seem to live such separate lives.

Let us return to Kevin:

CASE EXAMPLE

Kevin was a young professional man earlier presented who began psychoanalysis because of his persistent wish to cross-dress. He was quite distressed about this symptom, which had been with him as long as he remembered, certainly before his teens. He was an eager and cooperative patient who came dutifully to his appointments and was much pleased by his analytic work. Over time, his distress over cross-dressing remarkably diminished; he began a serious heterosexual relationship with a woman who was quite tolerant of his cross-dressing, and he made plans to move to another city. His analyst felt that the analysis was successful in most respects but not at all in terms of the initial, presenting symptom. Kevin moved away and later wrote to his analyst about how well he was doing, especially in his new venture of directing and organizing a cross-dressers' group. He claimed that his analysis had been invaluable to him in his new life and expressed gratitude to his analyst for the treatment.

This brief vignette is presented primarily to consider the question of evaluating this treatment as a success or a failure. No doubt, one would want a great deal more information about the conduct and content of the treatment to render a decision about a host of other considerations, but if restricted to this single query the conundrum is highlighted. A patient is treated with an endpoint of satisfaction but with no change in his initial complaint and no alteration of symptomatology. For some this is a cure, and for some this sounds like a failure. Indeed, for some theoretical approaches it qualifies as a success, and for others as a failure.[1]

Kevin's analyst felt the analysis was a failure because the symptom of cross-dressing was in no way altered. However, when this case was presented to a group of analysts, the majority of them felt the analysis was a success. The patient clearly felt himself to be a member of the group that determines just how a word will be used, and so he felt that he agreed with those who felt it a success. The resolution of these differences would seem possible if some standard of measurement could be acceptable to all and could be empirically tested (Rudolf et al., 2002). Some efforts in this direction have considered structural changes to be the crucial dimension in the determination of success or failure, and this is said to be measurable and thus to be a crucial criterion for a decision. One of the ways such change is measured is by a patient's retrospective evaluation of how he or she sees him or herself (Grande et al., 2009). Kevin felt that he saw himself differently and that this had had a lasting effect. His analyst saw it differently but would probably agree on a qualified or partial success. The matter is not settled.

THE CAUSE

The question about the reason for a failure follows after some consensus about what constitutes a success. Thus, a failed case is simply one that lacks the missing ingredient. This ingredient is often conceptualized as psychic structure and is thought to be a product of the analytic or therapeutic process. It should be able to be studied as to its presence or absence as the process unfolds from the development of the therapeutic alliance, to the establishment of a stable transference, and to the working-through period of the termination phase. The changes that occur according to other theoretical approaches can be explained in the vocabulary of each approach; these vocabularies are not interchangeable. In the case of failure, the most important question to be answered is that of cause. Of course, the very idea of "cause" assumes that something had or should have had an effect.

CASE EXAMPLE

Elizabeth came for her second analysis after the death of her husband, to whom she had been married for 30 years. Her first analysis was part of her own training to become a psychiatrist and seemed to be of little moment in her description of her life. The major topic of her concern that brought her to treatment was the grief that she experienced when her happy marriage was no more.

She insisted on a resumption of an analysis with her attending four times per week and lying on the couch. Most of the content of the treatment was about what a wonderful man she had been married to, and how she could never find anyone to replace him. She had a dream of sitting in a theater watching a play with an empty seat next to her. She found a group of like-minded women who were widows joined in regret over their loss and united in the determination that their loss was never to be replaced. Any suggestion that she was dwelling on the past was met with an irate defense of that state.

The analyst felt that the prolonged mourning of the dead husband, which had lasted several years, was a resistance to exploring other significant areas of depression, but any and all efforts at interpretation seemed to make no impact. Elizabeth was quite able to get angry at her analyst, but this seemed to do little to either provide relief or open other avenues of inquiry. All of the recommended therapeutic efforts to advance and resolve the mourning process were futile, and after a year or so Elizabeth decided to leave with the clear message that she was no better.

Elizabeth's analyst felt the attempted analysis was a failure, and he initially ascribed this failure to the patient's nonanalyzability; she was incapable of forming an alliance and a workable transference. However, he could not be sure. Perhaps he himself was incapable of offering his patient whatever was necessary for the accomplishment of those theoretical states, ones that everyone said were required for an analysis to prosper. He did often feel that Elizabeth should "get over it," but he never voiced that idea to her. Yet it was not impossible that she had felt this attitude was somehow in the air. When she was angry at him for not helping her more, he felt this was really directed at her husband for dying, but she would hear none of this. Perhaps another, more empathic analyst would have been able to be more sensitive and more convincing. However, this sort of second guessing is what followed every failure and seemed to be unresolvable. The analyst could even imagine a path that might well conclude with the conviction that his patient had really profited from the treatment by way of having someone to listen to her and to allow her to express her feelings about her husband. However, the analyst felt that that was merely twisting reality. Elizabeth had gotten no better, and that was a fact and not an opinion.

The cases of Kevin and Elizabeth touch upon the effort to answer our original questions that asked whether or not a case would qualify as a failure and what brought the failure about. This next case highlights the other questions about who was responsible and whether it could have been otherwise.

CASE EXAMPLE

Linda was a social worker who practiced psychotherapy and was married to a wealthy realtor. She did little of the former, and the latter allowed her to spend a great deal of money on shopping. She began an analysis with a well-known analyst, and she was never at a loss in naming and acknowledging his fame to others. Her marriage was unhappy, and much of her analysis focused on that problem along with the excessive shopping that she pursued. The analyst felt the two were connected, but that particular behavioral difficulty was quickly labeled an addiction and was treated by what she felt was a moralizing and chastising attitude by her analyst. Unfortunately, the shopping was in no way diminished by this approach. Her marriage, on the other hand, was handled in a seemingly more therapeutic manner, and this resulted in a trial separation and ultimate divorce from her husband.

Linda became friends with another woman who likewise had a severe shopping addiction that was handled in a much different manner in her own psychoanalytic therapy and that culminated in an apparent cessation of her shopping. Linda approached her analyst, asked why his technique seemed not to produce results, and asked whether he was familiar with and willing to try another technique. He dismissed both the technique and the possibility of his altering his own approach, and Linda continued to see him and to shop excessively.

No doubt, any reader of this brief vignette may have all sorts of questions about the issues that are presented. However, the point is not to offer a case for discussion but rather to offer the possibility that some cases of failure (and Linda's shopping addiction was recognized as having failed to be cured) are due to a reluctance or an inability to try a different approach. Sometimes this is due to an insistence on "staying the course" no matter how meritless this seems to be, and sometimes it is a result of not being able to utilize a different technical method. The latter is often a result of the insularity of our schools of thought.

DISCUSSION

The extreme points on the continuum of the lineup of failures range from considering each and every failed analytic case to be unique to the polar opposite position that insists they all result from a single and universal error. The latter might be something like a failure to be empathic or one or another countertransference problem. The former simply ends the conversation.

Another line of inquiry constructs a range of theories of pathology that runs from the *untreatable by any means* category to the *anything and everything works* group. The former remains hopeful of further research and innovative efforts. The latter tends to diminish playing favorites. The continuum does invite efforts to form particular categories of pathology that respond to particular therapeutic interventions. That direction is in sharp contrast to psychiatric differentiations that are based on phenomenology and are not necessarily in any way related to treatment.

A recent report from the *Minneapolis Star Tribune* (2009) announced that the "success rate at treating depression" for 54 participating clinics was "only about four percent" of patients considered in remission after 6 months of treatment. The usual response for such an unsuccessful rate of improvement is to try other medications, to increase the dosage of medications, or to add cognitive-behavioral therapy (CBT). Psychoanalytic or psychodynamic psychotherapy is routinely not considered ostensibly because of cost and time but more realistically because of lack of training in the reporting group. This failure to determine more specifically the best treatment for a particular patient is more or less the prevailing norm in the community of therapists. Psychoanalysis along with psychopharmacology operate with blinders in terms of recognizing alternative approaches.

Ideally, we aim to line up pathology with therapy. If that situation could be achieved, then the entire project of a careful evaluation of failure might be profitably launched. Unfortunately, we often operate with that ideal situation assumed, and we proceed with a critique guided by that assumption. Therefore, we look for empathic failure or countertransference issues as if they have universal applicability where they may be, in truth, of little relevance.

It may well be the case that many if not most cases of psychoanalytic failures are due to mistakes committed by the analyst. Such mistakes range from failure to create a therapeutic or working alliance, to failure to form a workable transference, on to countertransference problems and a host of failures to understand the patient. However, we must add to this list those failures that stem from a lack of clarity about the very definition of a failure, a lack of diagnostic evaluation as to treatability, and a lack of knowledge about alternative technical approaches.

We next need to better determine what expectations we may bring to bear on the undertaking of certain psychological conditions that may not be amenable to our efforts. The widening scope of analysis surely has its limits. An awareness of our limitations inevitably leads to a need to acquaint ourselves with what other theories and techniques have to offer. A casual review of today's psychiatric journals quickly reveals how a variety of treatments may be offered (say) for depression with a routine omission of psychodynamic psychotherapy (Brent et al., 2009). So, too, do our analytic journals describe treatment that is regularly restricted and insular, often with no recognition of CBT or medication. Once again, it is necessary to recognize that some disorders respond to a wide variety of interventions, and some to a very specific modality of treatment. We need to know the difference.

ENDNOTES

1. There are two opposing schools within the philosophy of language (Wanderer, 2005). The first school assumes that the central feature of language is its capacity to represent the way things are; the second assumes that language is best thought of as a set of social practices so that in order to understand how language works, we must attend to the uses to which sentences are put and the circumstances in which they are used. In terms of our effort to conceptualize failure, we need to recognize that it gains its meaning from the particular group that determines exactly how it will be used. There is no clear way that failure can become a fact or a truth except against a background of agreed-upon standards of evaluation or, better said, a normative scale. Only from that baseline, that set of social practice, can one derive the conclusion of a success or a failure. Certainly at times there will be an almost universal agreement on these words, but at other times the groups that develop the usage of these words may not themselves be able to agree on a suitable definition.

12

Me and Max*

A Misalliance of Goals

Many references have been made to the need for a clear and definitive decision about the goals of a treatment, be it psychotherapy or psychoanalysis. Over time, every therapist struggles with the proper consideration of a goal that fits a particular patient (e.g., does one have a limited goal, or is there a universal goal for every patient?). What is a common and perhaps unfortunate state of affairs is that the goals of the patient and the therapist often do not match. We have noted this in Chapter 11 in the case of Kevin, the cross-dresser, but it may be present in almost every case and may reflect a theoretical bias that often is unrecognized.

MAX

One of the burned-in memories of my lengthy life as an analytic candidate is of an event that took place in a case conference chaired by Maxwell Gitelson. Gitelson was a sort of crotchety and imposing man who was fairly humorless and could easily and honestly be characterized as opinionated. This particular moment of meaning of mine occurred when, to the best of my memory,

* This chapter originally appeared in *Psychoanalytic Quarterly*, 70, 2001, pp. 117–130. Reprinted with permission.

a student said something or other about either his and/or the patient's hope (and goal) that the patient would soon feel better. Gitelson proclaimed (rather than offered) his opinion that psychoanalysis was not meant to make people feel better or to relieve symptoms; rather, the goal of analysis was to allow patients to better understand themselves. Relief of symptoms was a sort of chance byproduct of such understanding, but it was definitely *not* the goal of analysis. Nor should any psychoanalyst pursue that essentially secondary effort.

My silent reaction to Gitelson's "Bah, humbug" appraisal of symptom relief was my own "Bah, humbug," because I was convinced that almost everyone I knew in analysis wanted to feel better, and if self-understanding was what had to be swallowed, then that medicine could and would be endured, but it was hardly the goal that I personally would rank as number one. It seemed clear that one person's goal was just not properly or necessarily made for another. Rather than one size fitting all, it seemed that the goals of the patients, the goals of the analysts, and the goals of the field of psychoanalysis might well lie in separate areas of concern. They need not be in opposition, but they surely are not and cannot be reduced to identical significance and importance.

The combination of my desire to be a good student, plus my near-total intimidation by Gitelson, allowed me over time to adopt his singular goal as mine. I periodically and often surprisingly found myself saying and even believing that the goal of analysis was self-understanding, especially when my patients would point out that I was not helping much with their psychic distress. I could readily recognize the comfort that this adopted stance offered, inasmuch as it allowed me to cast myself as someone in pursuit of this more noble effort of a variation of "truth," rather than settling for the lesser metal of mere comfort and relief. Also, the analyst's view of symptom relief as a happy though accidental companion of analysis enables the analyst to achieve a feeling of personal pleasure without the encumbrance of satisfying someone else's (the patient's) wishes. In this way, I found myself allied with what I imagined were the more lofty aims of the field, rather than joined with those of the individual patient: selfish but safe.

Sooner or later, one must surely realize that concern over the proper goals for what one achieves or what discipline one espouses is basically a moral issue. The pursuit of doing well readily collapses into doing the right thing, and so a conflict occurs, at times, between making the patient feel better and, say, satisfying Freud's (1933) axiom of "Where id was, there shall ego be" (p. 80). Unless the satisfaction of the axiom yields an equal degree of contentment for the patient, one cannot reduce the latter to a byproduct of the former. The relief of symptoms and the happiness of the patient become the goals, according to this moral stance, and the goal of self-understanding sort of trots alongside. One could, of course, eliminate the problem if these two or three goals always emerged and then merged together, but we are regularly haunted by analyzed patients who claim that they feel no better, alongside happy ones who seem quite psychologically opaque. My loyalty to Gitelson was severely tried.

CHARLES

My next memory, a bit less severely etched, comes from another teacher, Charles Kligerman, who was anything but crotchety but probably equally opinionated. He would regularly say that analyzed people are just different from nonanalyzed ones. He would also pronounce this with a certain sense of the former belonging to a very exclusive club, and with the secondary message that one would do well to limit one's acquaintances, friends, and certainly spouses to that membership. Putting aside this seductive elitism, Kligerman's position made it clear that analysis did something that was lasting and was more than just freeing someone from psychic pain, because that latter quality would never by itself lead to this exclusive club admittance. Therefore, the goal of analysis involved some significant alteration in the patient, one that went beyond symptom relief and perhaps even beyond that ephemeral state of understanding. It made one a different person—and, at least to some, a better one as well.

Somehow, the goals were beginning to become better demarcated, although perhaps not in the way Max and I might have wished for. They were not singular in that they had to satisfy a multiplicity of needs. But perhaps the most striking alteration or addition to this original and somewhat encapsulated version of goals offered by my mentor was that the change was not limited to the patient, but seemed to extend to the analyst as well. That is to say that the practitioners of analysis are different, both because of their personal analyses and because they practice the somewhat noble enterprise of turning out special people. To combine the views of my two mentors might well lead to one being overwhelmed by elitism, as well as by the altitude of this rarified atmosphere.

The challenge that presented itself to me was that of reconciling or somehow unifying what seemed to be a threefold set of goals: that of self-understanding, of relief of discomfort, and of a lasting or relatively permanent change or enhancement of value. Each of these three seemed essential, and each seemed connected to the others. Thus, the focus upon one or another should contain some element that would lead to the others. Without in any way denying the multitude of subsidiary benefits of treatment, which could range from a happier marriage to a more fulfilling sex life, these three endpoints should be all-encompassing. So now we shall examine each in turn.

SELF-UNDERSTANDING

The dominance of the ego and the accumulation of insight into one's unconscious, taken together, are assumed to lead to a body of knowledge that enables one to comprehend one's self differently. This difference may take the form of a narrative of one's history or, on other occasions, might narrow in on a retelling of a more focused event, such as a particular moment of trauma. Patients surely differ in the manner in which they reflect back upon their analyses. No matter how much one insists upon analysis being an activity in which the participants engage in narration (Schafer, 1992), or one of the recovery of memory (Fonagy, 1999), these are more properly seen as one or another *form* of the procedure, rather than as the fundamental goal. There can be little doubt that some patients prefer telling their life stories, some wish to concentrate on the here and now with little reference to personal history, and some seem peculiarly devoted to elaborate Proustian reminiscence. That such a personal preference is regularly seen to match the preference of the analyst alerts us to the value of looking for this particular form of the goal of analysis as sometimes lying outside the essence of the process.

Consider the following patient:

CASE EXAMPLE

A young professional man entered analysis with the clearly defined and stated aim of getting married. He claimed to have had a host of involvements with marriageable women, but not to have done much more than living with one for a few months. That particular experience was characterized by emotions ranging from discontent to disgust, with not a hint of a wish for this couple of roommates to remain together. Yet he insisted that he longed for marriage to the right woman, and he hoped that analysis would realize that possibility.

I shall not detail the conduct of this analysis, save to say that somewhere along the line, he did marry, but long after he had dropped that issue as crucial to his life as an analysand. What memories he did recover seemed minimal, and as Alexander (1940/1964) long ago suggested, these were more confirmatory than revealing. I believe that the patient and I would be hard-pressed to recount a detailed new version of his life as well. Indeed, most of his analysis had to do with his father, and concentrated not surprisingly on the minutiae of the transference reflective of this.

Toward the end of his analysis, there was no doubt that the patient saw himself differently; thereafter, almost everything problematic in his life, from a telephone call to his mother, to the loss of money on an apparently promising stock, led to his subjecting himself to self-scrutiny. His psychic life was of two parts: The first was composed of a relative ease regarding events and relationships with others, and the second of an intense self-reflection upon anything that represented conflict or difficulty. (It should not be necessary to underscore that this division is not true of everyone, inasmuch as many of us are frequently carefree, whereas others seem never to be free of concern and worry.) My patient regularly reviewed and reflected upon the puzzle of everyday life, and he did so in a manner and with a method that was clearly a miniaturized version of his analytic experience.

I think it safe to conclude that the self-understanding that was facilitated in this analysis was a product of the personalities of both of us, and that it could be characterized by using a variety of theoretical lexicons. That I spoke a certain language, which my patient over time made his own, should not be seen as mere brainwashing. His way of thinking about himself during the analysis would often begin with him announcing, "I know that you would say…" I took this as a form of both identification and differentiation. Indeed, one might well say that my patient began by understanding me, and then moved on to an understanding of himself. I take this feature as essential: The gradual dissolution of the transference should over time reveal the analyst to the patient.

The greatest obstacle to this hoped-for sequence is often the unwitting or unnecessary *self-revelation of the analyst*. The discovery of what the world, any world, is like may follow the guidelines or map of another, but it is not to be equated with a carbon copy of the other. This analysis ended with each of us changing and yet remaining quite different persons. The outstanding feature for the patient was his newfound capacity to puzzle over his life's ups and downs (i.e., his personal form of self-reflection).

RELIEF OF SYMPTOMS

Another patient reported to me after a year of analysis that she felt much better in comparison to how she had felt a year earlier, but could in no way say just what her analysis had accomplished. This feature of feeling better is a happy companion to psychotherapy, psychopharmacology, and even the ordinary occurrences of everyday life. Everything from a good night's sleep to winning the lottery can be capable of eliciting this sort of self-report of contentment, but only a few persons seem able to sustain this desired endpoint. No doubt, a certain amount of ongoing maintenance in the form of the above-mentioned self-analytic or self-reflective work is essential for the sustaining of this feeling of being better, but that seems not to be the whole story. Just as I might give credit to one or more of my teachers who studied and wrote about post-termination self-analysis (Robbins & Schlessinger, 1983), I owe my debt for knowledge about the more lasting effects of analytic improvement to Heinz Kohut.

Kohut was often at odds with those who emphasized the role of self-analysis following one's work in a therapeutic analysis. He felt that the establishment of meaningful selfobject relationships, or the opening of empathic connections between persons, was the foundation of analytic cure (Kohut, 1984). Therefore, one need not be concerned with self-analytic work, save for moments of disruptive breaks in these empathic connections. The availability and deployment of selfobjects were the essentials for navigating through life, and psychic health was equivalent to this dual capacity. Thus, Kohut looked upon self-analysis as evidence more of an incomplete analysis than of the ongoing maintenance of analytic benefits. If one had established a firm and lasting sense of self-cohesion, then there need be few occasions for the self-reflective work necessary to repair an empathic disruption. Or so the story goes.

My own ecumenical bent was to join the two issues of self-cohesion and self-reflection, inasmuch as I remained ever short of perfection, and given that most of my patients were wedded to regular self-reflection. No one in my caseload had achieved the sought-for ideal state of persistent selfobject sustenance alone. Although this was a desirable point of personal achievement, such an ideal state was equally often elusive. For some patients, it was overwhelmingly elusive, whereas for others, self-reflection was an equal rarity. Once again, the mix of goals among my patients reflected the complexity of an interaction between two complex entities: the patient and the analyst, along with these two elements—self-cohesion and self-reflection—of supposed cure. The patient who reported feeling better after a year of therapy had no doubt made the necessary connection to allow for a firm sense of self-solidity with her selfobjects. But would it last?

THE LASTING VALUE

The lasting value of feeling better is the product of an underlying change that is attributable to something called *psychic structure*. Although this may be described and developed in a variety of ways, it underscores a way of talking about one's stability over time. This stability may be thought of as an enabler of both self-reflection and the relief of symptoms. Although it may seem intangible and even tautological, it is the theoretical convenience that we employ to characterize the improvement associated with analytic goals.

This gain or growth in psychic structure is often claimed to be equivalent to the ordinary processes of normal development. More properly, however, it may be thought of as analogous to development. Normal persons are not analyzed persons. Achieving a solid sense of connection with one's selfobjects, like gaining insight into the contents of one's unconscious, cannot be readily equated with the process of a normal child's development. For the former—achieving enduring connections—there is an ease of selfobject relationships in development that is rarely the case in analyzed adults, who are at best able to cautiously and carefully choose particular others to whom they can connect. For the latter, knowing one's unconscious, it is a failure of repression that reveals the unconscious to an adult who is most successful if his or her drives are neutralized or sublimated. Such nonneurotics claim not insight, but ignorance.

But any psychoanalytic theory can be used to distinguish and describe the analyzed person as different from the unanalyzed but nonneurotic one, and all such theories ultimately point to a crucial distinction of some sort. In a nutshell, analysis *adds* something to the person who is analyzed, and this addition, no matter how one speaks of it, becomes a lasting and distinguishing characteristic. *Psychic structure* is the catchword for what is added. It is by way of this concept that one is able to consider the significance of the time axis in the achievements of analysis. Change that lasts, or *enduring function*, reflects this underlying something that offers stability and sustenance. Now perhaps we are able to weld together and join the three measures of analytic accomplishment.

ALWAYS ANALYZING

My now-married patient described in this chapter, who is presently gripped by the sheer curiosity of living, once complained to me that he was jealous of those friends and acquaintances who seemed to be happy—or even unhappy—but who had no concern as to the origins of their psychic status. Indeed, they seemed to move through life without really thinking about it. In a way, he was envious of their unconcern, and he often wished that more things did *not* matter so much to him. It was not that he worried—although he would readily admit to that—but rather that he was ever curious. And he was convinced that his analysis had given him this affliction of persistent puzzling. As glad as he might be about his ability to better see himself, it was also very much as though a chronic illness had been bestowed upon him. What a burden to have—as if life were some sort of continuing mystery story whose clues were unending. However, as any lover of mysteries will tell you, following clues is a lovely addiction.

To borrow a phrase from the eminent French philosopher Paul Ricoeur (1992), we are able to, and we should, see "oneself as another." This perception, which takes place as we step to one side of where we are usually situated, is distorted by all of the prejudices and preconceptions of subjectivity. We may, however, gain a modicum of objectivity with the aid of psychoanalysis. We do so not by sharing another's (i.e., the analyst's) subjectivity, which, although to be valued in part, is possibly merely another person's opinion. The whole point of analysis must lie in the fact that it is a body of knowledge based upon fundamental principles and ideas about transference and the unconscious.

So my patient must see him or herself through this lens, regardless of whether he or she is more or less successful as an autobiographer. Because this autobiography is coauthored, its credibility rests upon faithfulness to analysis, rather than on personal clarity or concealment. As a patient, one explains one's self to oneself by way of psychoanalytic understanding, while perhaps failing, more or less, as a writer of fiction, omitting something that might be more interesting and/or fascinating but less faithful to our field. The roteness of analytic lore may make for dullness of revelation, inasmuch as self-scrutiny returns again and again to situations highlighted in the treatment and faithful to our theory.

IMMUNIZATION

The return of a patient who has completed a course of analysis, now with either a concomitant return of symptoms and problems or a whole new set of difficulties, seems to happen often enough for it to be claimed as an inevitability in the life of every analyst. With this return, there is often an implicit registering of a complaint, one that suggests a disappointment that the analysis did not quite work, did not protect the patient from further difficulties, and/or did not bestow a sort of lifelong immunity. It is as if to say that all future troubles are essentially a return of the old ones, in either the same or a different form, for at heart, the expected solution turned out to be nothing but a Band-Aid. This implicit complaint seeks a voice, despite the fact that time has passed, circumstances have changed, events that no one could have foreseen have occurred, and, quite likely, self-scrutiny has diminished and faded.

Although we may embrace the concept of structural change as underlying analytic effectiveness, we may have to strain to account for the continued frailty of our discharged patients. We rationalize our limitations with portentous statements about the limits of analytic treatment, citing problems inherent in libidinal stickiness, or making irrelevant references to biological givens—all the while aiming to remove ourselves and the analytic method from the equation. Perhaps it is our own sales pitch, the one offered to me by one of my teachers, about the very special status of analysis that has led us into this illusion of a perfect psychic paradise. Analytic treatment, like politics, is local. It can make no claim to permanently insulate a person from the unexpected, innumerable vicissitudes of life, because, as much as one would hope, the neuroses of childhood are not complete explanations for the trials of adulthood. The two-part explanation for the successful ending of an analysis discussed in this chapter, that of self-analysis and of open empathic connections, leads us into a clearer picture of the incompleteness of the theory of infantile neurosis and the resulting potential for analyzed patients to encounter continuing problems.

FORM VERSUS CONTENT

By advocating the making conscious of the unconscious, Freud's axiom mentioned earlier implied that psychic health was inextricably tied to insight, that knowledge was empowering, and that this new power was curative. Simply put, this is a "content cure," wherein the exposure of the contents of the unconscious enables a change that, although later elaborated with various forms of energetic variations, is fundamentally based upon knowing. The reexperience of the conflicts of infancy and childhood, classically thought of as infantile neurosis, should allow one as an adult to see things differently. To be sure, this reexperience requires a full affective charge to qualify as a valid one, but the original foundation was that of revisiting an earlier trauma with later *adult* competence. The transparency of the analyst, even in its guise of a neutral position (Baker, 2000), insists that an earlier situation is and must be reenacted in treatment, and that this can be effected only by allowing history to repeat itself within the analysis. Such repetition involves the analyst not interfering with the emergence of unconscious material, because this material remains the root cause of the neurosis.

This is not the case with the explanation derived from "form" rather than content. Here it is not the "what" that is the problem, but the "how." For this type of patient, we shift our explanation from conflict over unfortunate discord to deficits resulting from faulty development. To be sure, one can readily see that every conflict somehow implies some sort of a deficit, in repression, neutralization of drives, ego weakness, or any variant of alternative theoretical explanations. No matter the theory, one may still comprehend a difference between the patient who needs insight and the one who needs more, regardless of how one chooses to characterize or pathologize the latter. This second patient is the one who seems to gain relief from the regularity of visits, the listening of the analyst, the feeling of being understood—all those ingredients that are lumped together under the unhappy wastebasket term *the relationship*. This is the patient who may, upon recalling his or her analysis, speak of the analyst's tone of voice, the feelings aroused upon entering the room, the long and difficult termination punctuated by an occasional revisit, and the very expected Christmas card exchange. Often, this is also the patient about whom we may feel a bit guilty or embarrassed: the one for whom some administrative boundary had been breached.

The thesis that I wish to offer flows from my earlier conviction that one size does not fit all, that analysis means and does different things for and to different people, and that the straitjacket-like nature of our rules leads to a rigidity in the determination of our goals. Every patient has an individual mix of self-reflection coupled with empathic connections, and one is not to be prized over the other. Indeed, this variability of needs carries over to different patients at different times, and is certainly true of one patient with different analysts. So it is only in the most general sense that we can meld together the activity of self-reflection and meaningful connections with others to fashion an endpoint applicable to any single patient. It is, however, advisable to keep in mind that we can never precisely divide an analysis into the convenient categories that we may sketch out. It is not true that we can determine exactly when we will deal with transference configurations and when with new development, or that at a particular time we have a real relationship, and at another time a visitor from the past. We are never so lucky.

DISCUSSION

If one were to ask a primary care physician, a college teacher, and an auto mechanic what the goals of their occupations are, they would probably all preface their responses with "It all depends." In a way, those are dreaded and dreadful words, hiding the fact that the respondents first require some input from the questioner in order to shape and determine the answer. Not so with the plumber called in to unplug your sink, the teacher of first-year French, and the internist treating a specific patient with pneumonia. The easy answers involve focused efforts at fixing a specific problem; the hard ones relate to general aims of amelioration.

Psychoanalysis does not enjoy focused fixes. As much as we would like it to be otherwise, we are haunted by vagueness. Yet this atmosphere of uncertainty makes analysis the rich field that it is, inasmuch as, if every patient has an oedipal problem, then we are too much the plumber. "Never knowing for sure" is the proper place for our own "It all depends" and our own insistence on the individual patient finding his or her own goals.

The supposed grammatical error of my title comes from a linguistic choice. It is meant to state itself in the accusative case (i.e., as the object of a verb). It is intended to convey what the goals of psychoanalysis mean to me and to Max, because Max and I continue to think quite differently, just as I continue to live with uncertainty. The vibrancy of analysis derives both from its fundamental thesis of transference and the unconscious, and from the indeterminate shape of each of these fundamentals. To combine the two—fundamentals plus change—results in our being able to specify the goals of psychoanalysis with the addendum of some phrase like "as of now" or "for the time being," alongside "for this particular person." In this way, we can and should embrace the vagueness of our work. Max was a great teacher because he was so sure of himself—and, paradoxically, could produce a student who could live happily with a multitude of opinions.

13

Empathy and Failure*

It is a somewhat common event at psychoanalytic meetings to hear a case presentation discussed by a number of commentators of different theoretical backgrounds. Each of the discussants manages to explain the clinical material from his or her own vantage point, and rather than a congenial meeting of minds there usually is a hardening of opinions. I recall one such occasion in which it seemed to be clear to everyone that the patient was getting worse with this particular analytic approach, and although other suggestions were made by proponents of different technical ideas, the leading representative of the extant theory being applied solemnly declared that everything was going as it should and the patient was doing just fine. Interestingly, the arguments that might have ensued were not voiced, and an aura of resignation descended on the assemblage as if to say that everyone was entitled to his or her opinion. That is often the conclusion of such meetings, with the hope that some of the unaffiliated listeners might come away convinced that analyst A was more persuasive than B or C. and so join in support of that set of beliefs.

Inasmuch as it appears to be true that most accomplished supporters of just about any psychoanalytic or psychodynamic theory

---

* Portions of this chapter, as well as Chapter 14, appeared in an earlier form in *Journal of the American Psychoanalytic Association*, 59(2), April 2011, pp. 289–311.

can make a compelling case to explain just about any patient, there still may be a way to make sense of the fact that they do not enjoy uniform success in treatment. What is needed is to separate the explanatory power of the theory from the efficacy of the application of the theory. When listening to the case of the patient who was getting worse, one could readily be convinced of how the theory might explain what was happening but hardly be convinced that this was doing the patient much good. It is always quite difficult initially to agree with the story but to disagree with the application. Where it might be hoped and expected that the technique would automatically flow out of the theory, we routinely see how this is simply not true. It may at times be more accurate to say that some technical interventions are considered to be true to the theory but not helpful to the patient, and so the truth of the theory really should refer to its relevance to the patient. Thus when the aforementioned expert declared that the patient was doing just fine, he had lost sight of the gap that must be bridged between the wisdom of the theory and its beneficial impact on the patient.

All of the working approaches to psychoanalytic and psycho-therapeutic can be divided into a part devoted to understanding the patient and another part directed to doing something about what was understood. Though it is a sad truth that many (Fink, 2010) may choose to dismiss the crucial point of understanding, there really can be no chance of helping a patient without first understanding what is there to be helped. This, of course, is not to say that the understanding per se is what is helpful, only that it allows one to initiate a process that may be so.

One of the great arguments in psychoanalytic self psychology is waged over the status of empathy either as a process of data gathering or as a therapeutic tool in its own right. When a patient is understood by a therapist, is that fact helpful on its own or must the patient *feel* understood in order to benefit? There is a tendency by many to collapse the two phenomena and so to automatically consider understanding as ameliorative on the face of it. It may be necessary to further distinguish the communication of understanding to a patient as equally necessary for a certain subgroup of patients. It is probably likely that many patients are "understood" by many therapists and not much helped because of these elements not being distinguished. In what follows are extended discussions of the possible problematic status of empathy.

The problems and centrality devoted to empathy and empathic disruptions are part and parcel of the theory and vocabulary of self psychology, but they are by no means confined to that perspective. These are meant only to be illustrative of one approach to studying what was earlier discussed as mistakes. They range from a failure to do something that should be done to doing what should not be done to doing something wrong. The problems involving empathy are the errors of everyday life.

The popularity of the concept of empathy along with that of the newfound interest in mirror neurons has led to both an effort to find a neurological basis for empathy (Gallese, 2008) and a vigorous counterreaction to any form of premature linkage between the mind and the brain (Vivona, 2009). This chapter aims to present a particular psychoanalytic perspective on the term *empathy* along with a suggested modifying adjective.

In 1987, Lauren Wispe wrote a "History of the Concept of Empathy" and thereby demonstrated how the concept of empathy has changed over time. As a start we can use the definition of the *American Heritage Dictionary,* in which it is defined as "understanding so intimate that the feelings, thoughts, and motives of one are readily comprehended by another." M. F. Basch (1983) modified that definition when he wrote that the word *empathy* needed to be tied to the word *understanding* in order to properly consider its role in psychoanalysis, and by his added emphasis on the role of affect he underscored an operational definition of empathy. Empathic understanding is a process by which one person gets to know another person. Over time, phrases such as *mature empathy* or *generative empathy* (Schafer, 1968) have been introduced to differentiate it from mere attunement or a host of value-laden terms that may be designed to reflect primarily an altruistic motive. To now introduce another modification to a term that seems to allow both a number of definitions and a plethora of modifiers is an effort to distinguish a process that psychoanalysis holds in a special status: sustained empathy.

Although the literature on empathy, no matter how one defines it, is enormous, often no effort is made to distinguish what one might call "ordinary empathy" or "common sense empathy" from "sustained empathy" (Araqno, 2008). This latter concept was one championed by Heinz Kohut (1971) in his explication of self psychology, but it is regularly collapsed into some form of a general collection of ideas either about one's being empathic or else in teaching empathy or in having empathy for certain specific affect states. My goals in this chapter are to try to distinguish between these two conceptualizations of empathy—the ordinary and often instantaneous, and the sustained—and then to elaborate some distinctions peculiar to sustained empathy. The first task can be simplified by invoking a comparison between a single snapshot and a video; in other words, a timeline is introduced to separate what seems to characterize most discussions and definitions of empathy in the ordinary sense from what distinguishes the lengthy immersion of one person in another's psychological state. The quality of this latter condition (i.e., what makes it unique) as well as the implications of the effort are the aims of this chapter. Empathy over time is a qualitatively different phenomenon, more than the mere quantitative idea of temporal measurement would suggest. Understanding another person over time leads to a sequence of events, and that sequence for psychoanalysis offers a particular form of explanation. The underlying thesis is that without sustained empathy, failure may well ensue.

MEANINGS OF SUSTAINED EMPATHY

R. G. Collingwood is the philosopher of history who is credited with the insistence that all ideas, all facts, must be historicized. He felt that the past can be understood only by discovering the intentions of particular persons at particular times (Inglis, 2009). Thus, one must put ideas in context, as well as include the persons who capture these ideas and the stories of those persons. Darwin, of course, taught us that all persons are results of a long series of historic events (Coyne, 2009). Sigmund Freud is the preeminent voice for stressing our need to see how someone got to where he or she is, yet we often read of being empathic with another person as if it were a slice of time rather than an unfolding story. This is especially true of much of the neurological study of empathy.

A recent article on electrical activity in the human brain demonstrated neuronal activation in Broca's area for speech production. It added the caveat,

> As is known for neurons in the visual cortex, the specific contribution of Broca's area may well vary with time, as a consequence of the different dynamic cortical networks in which it is embedded at different time slices. This fits well with the finding that Broca's area is not language specific, but is also recruited in the service of other cognitive domains, such as music and action and with the finding that its contribution to language processing crosses the boundaries of semantics, syntax, and phonology. (Hagoort & Levelt, 2009, pp. 372–373)

This echoes the contention that the data gathered by empathic connection or indeed by any means must be seen both in context and over time. Different time slices are but snapshots toward encompassing a complex set of meaning. The "here and now" is often a moment in time that may well be interesting but is best seen as a gateway portal to an arena of understanding. At times, the "here and now" as well is accessed only by way of sustained empathy, but it regularly requires a place in an ongoing sequence of meanings. This is the first aspect of sustained empathy; it is a sequence of events and emotions and is never singular. The second aspect has to do with the impact of sustained empathy. A few case representations will follow. There is no doubt that the thesis may well appear simple and obvious to some. The point of the exercise is to underscore the fact that empathy usually but not always extends along time, whereas brain studies are more often than not representative of a moment in time.

Psychoanalysts approach case material differently than those who are not analytically oriented, and this approach is often described as one involving hermeneutics or the science of interpretation. Its process is termed the *hermeneutic circle*. The process begins with the fact that we routinely know what we are looking for, or as Martin Heidegger, the father of hermeneutics, would say: Interpretation is grounded in a fore-conception (1927/1946, p. 141). The process that is suggested to achieve this grounding is a threefold one whose constituents are called (a) fore-having, (b) fore-sight, and (c) fore-conception. This involves (a) a tentative knowing of what is to be uncovered or disclosed, followed by (b) an approach that makes things comprehensible, and then (c) a grounding in a definite conception. These are the steps of the circle, and the circle is the structure of meaning (Goldberg, 2004).

This case is presented to illustrate how one listens both over time and with time in mind to gather meaning and so to participate in the hermeneutic circle.

CASE EXAMPLE

Charles was a 52-year-old homosexual who lived alone and had no lasting significant partners. He came hesitantly into treatment because of a feeling that he was missing out on life. He was the fourth child of 10 children born to a Korean mother who spoke little English and a Caucasian father described as distant and aloof. After a series of weekly visits, it was suggested that Charles begin an analysis, a suggestion to which he readily agreed. Initially the analysis went quite smoothly, and Charles claimed to feel comfortable and hopeful. After one month, Charles reported a dream that was interpreted to the mutual agreement of both Charles and his analyst. However, the day following this interpretation Charles insisted on sitting up. He challenged his analyst with being up to something insidious, and announced that he was quitting his analysis. Inexplicably, after a short absence Charles returned to analysis and resumed with the calmer conduct of an analysand who was content with the process and the results. Along with this claim of contentment and improvement, after another presentation of a dream and its successful interpretation, there occurred a similar set of behaviors with accusations and separation. This sequence of calm followed by a severe change of emotional state with subsequent recovery only to repeat itself presented a befuddlement to the analyst, who could see general and gradual improvement only to be met by a seeming undoing of all that had been accomplished.

When this case was presented to a conference to discuss how the issue of its analyzability was so mistaken and just why the treatment was so punctuated with both hope and despair, someone suggested an explanation. This consisted of an effort to be empathic across time. The hypothesis that was offered could certainly not be confirmed but consisted of the possibility that the patient was demonstrating what it was like to be one of 10 children and to have his closeness to his mother repeatedly interrupted by the birth of another child. No sooner was he content than his life was turned upside down. Thus, one listener chose a developmental conception to guide her listening.

This case is not presented as a necessarily accurate portrayal of this patient but rather as a reminder that we do regularly employ empathy along a timeline, and we think of cases in a narrative fashion. When the patient sat up and behaved in what the analyst termed a "paranoid" manner, one could be empathic with his rage, and one could conceptualize it as a changed emotional state following an interpretation. However, being empathic in the "here and now" is but an entrance into the overall task of understanding. The hermeneutic circle, which is often referred to as representing the activity of psychoanalysis (Goldberg, 2004), is seen as a back-and-forth process that is modified by each of the participants. The ability to sustain one's empathy during the course of the analytic process allows the analyst to replicate the history of an individual's developmental life. Of course, this is not definitive as such, but it serves to distinguish psychoanalysis as an interpretive science that employs sustained empathy.

CASE EXAMPLE

After her analyst moved to another city, Cynthia was urged to resume analysis without delay, and she did so without a moment's hesitation. She presented herself to her new analyst as a grief-stricken patient who had lost someone of great importance to her and whose loss seemed to generate an intense anger that surprisingly soon became directed at her new analyst. This replacement analyst felt that he could be empathic with this new patient's rage and bereavement, but Cynthia would have none of this "empathy," which she scoffed at and ridiculed. Indeed, she soon revealed that she was not so much angry at the supposed unfortunate departure of her old analyst, but rather she had constructed a complex justification for her rage at her new and seemingly innocent present analyst.

Cynthia's new analyst readily moved from his empathic stance of an attempt at understanding the anger of his new patient to one of puzzlement along with his own anger. Once again, we see that empathy is never a matching of feelings and the hoped-for understanding that results but rather is a complex configuration that is a story told over time.

The story that did explain Cynthia's rage was revealed after some period of treatment and both surprised and dismayed her new analyst. Cynthia felt that her old analyst was not helping her at all, yet she was completely unable to extricate herself from him. She had constructed an imaginary scenario that consisted of her new analyst or someone like him interfering with the ongoing process of her old analysis and either setting the old analyst straight or else rescuing her from this unfortunate entanglement. She was thus justifiably (to her) angry at her new analyst's failure to rescue her. Of course, this particular fantasy could not possibly have a basis in fact, nor could it have been readily accessed by an immediate empathic stance.

Empathy may at times offer an entry point into the hermeneutic circle, but it may also serve as a totally erroneous door to nowhere. Empathy is usually layered as well as sequential. Beneath Cynthia's anger was her severe and painful disappointment at the failure of her analyst and also at her parents. There is no way one could gain access to this experience save by the analytic process, and this necessarily takes place over time. Thus her analyst had to, in turn, be empathic with her rage, her life experiences leading to her fantasy, and her subsequent disappointment. Thus, one needs to sustain and modify empathy to achieve understanding. Empathy changes over time, and alone it explains little. Empathy is the data that must be carefully organized in terms of cause and effect, and sequencing and goals (Goldberg, 2004). If seen in isolation, it is but a form of attunement or affective resonance that need have no meaning on its own. Its universality should not be taken to be indicative of any particular therapeutic benefit, inasmuch as here too one must not see it in isolation. Empathy can be good, bad, or indifferent, and it is to this we now turn once again, keeping in mind the need for it to be lasting and often beneficial.

CASE EXAMPLE

Mike came into treatment in the midst of a contentious divorce that became resolved only after months of acrimony. The marriage might properly be characterized as one of Mike taking care of everything up and to including making dinner when he returned from work, whereas his wife merely did as little as possible. Of course, this was Mike's own characterization of his marriage, but I doubt that it was very far from the truth. I became more convinced of this state of affairs when Mike told of incident after incident of his competence. He carefully explained to the car mechanic exactly what was wrong with a malfunctioning foreign car. And he was right, and the mechanic was impressed and grateful. He patiently explained to a coworker how to organize a particularly complex set of ideas, and, once again, he showed his extraordinary ability to solve complex problems. In all of these examples, and there were many, Mike was exceedingly polite and gracious, although in his recounting of these stories of his super-competence Mike was less than charitable toward his listeners, who ranged from positions best described as pupils, colleagues, or adversaries. Mostly as a whole, they were tolerated.

It was not difficult to empathize with Mike's feeling of superiority over his incompetent fellows. He was sometimes exasperated, sometimes pleased, sometimes enraged, and sometimes even surprised at his own cleverness. Mike could discuss just how he affected others, including his now ex-wife along with the new women that he began courting. These discussions led to Mike's recounting of a childhood that seemed to be representative of two dominant traits. One was that of learning from an uncle how to fix all sorts of complex machines. The other was of being absolutely terrible at sports from striking out at baseball game after game to never really learning how to swim. One strand was of competence, and the other of failure. Beneath Mike's never-ending showing others how to do things was the little boy who could hardly do anything very well. Getting in touch with the helpless child that Mike continually wished to disown was an empathic stance that was achieved over time. It lay under or hidden from the extremely competent person who could more immediately be apprehended and recognized. When Mike himself was able to be in touch with his own fear of his own incompetence, he became almost apologetic about knowing so much.

THE THERAPEUTIC EFFECT OF SUSTAINED EMPATHY

We have seen sustained empathy as aiming not for a moment of meaning but as an extended explanation of sometimes contradictory and hidden meanings.

The therapeutic effect of this sustained empathy has to do with the impact of empathy on the one who is the target of the empathy, sometimes called the *empathasand*. There is much evidence in day-to-day practice that people feel better when they feel understood, and there are a multitude of explanations for this positive state. Different psychoanalytic theories offer different explanations ranging from the release of the repressed, ascribed to classical theory, to a host of other such possibilities. However, there does seem to be a difference between the pleasure that one receives when (say) a dream is interpreted and so seems to make sense, and that of the ongoing contentment and satisfaction experienced when one feels connected and understood over time. Agosta (2009) made the claim that one gains one's own feeling of humanness from another human being, and so he declared that "empathy is the foundation of human community where 'community' means 'being with one another in human interrelation'" (p. xiv).

This connectedness of one person to one or more others is to be considered in both its short-term and long-term effects. They seem both similar and different. Short-term effects are commonly thought of as a cognitive achievement such as when one gains insight following interpretation. Long-term effects need not have a significant cognitive dimension but may occur when one feels a connection to a person or a group that is seen as sustaining or fulfilling. In truth, a multitude of studies outside of psychoanalysis have been conducted to demonstrate the positive therapeutic effects that result from this feeling of belonging or participating.

The nonanalytic studies that have concerned themselves with the benefits of human relatedness range from those that measure the biological mechanisms that explain the positive association between social integration and physical health (Hawkley & Cacioppo, 2003) to the studies of particular diseases and social relationships (Bae, Hashimoto, Karlson, Liang, & Daltroy, 2001). They also extend to the hormonal biochemical issues involved in the connecting of one person to others (Van Anders & Watson,

2007). There is quite an accumulation of research and data on the full range of the issues involving the positive as well as the negative effects of social relationships (Cacioppo et al., 2002). What is lacking in all of the data is an adequate psychoanalytic or even psychological explanation of the significant correlation between emotional well-being and social networks. Every level but the unconscious is mentioned and measured, but sustained empathy and its psychological impact are bypassed. Basch (1983) felt it necessary to use the term *empathic understanding* to emphasize the psychological, but our use of the term *sustained empathy* is really shorthand for sustained empathic understanding.

Because sustained empathy is a cornerstone of psychoanalytic self psychology, it is no surprise that one of the best but not the only explanation for its therapeutic effect comes from that theoretical vision. The theory that is proposed is one built around the selfobject or another person serving as a fundamental part of the self. Thus, the person utilizes others as psychic structure. The person is constituted and sustained by these relationships to others; therefore, self psychology is essentially a one-person psychology that explains how others become aspects of one's self. Deficiencies in one's self become filled by others, and so a selfobject relationship leads to a feeling of self-integration. One is made whole by others.

If one considers a social relationship such as marriage and evaluates the positive and negative effects of such a connection, the results can be seen or explained at many levels. For instance, married men are more likely to adhere to recommendations for screening colonoscopy than unmarried men (Denberg, Melhado, Coombes, Beaty, & Berman, 2005). If one studies this level of interaction at the most obvious level, then one may miss the content of the psychological level. One person might say that his or her spouse will be pleased or proud and may mirror the activity of such adherence. Such connections may be enduring and maintain those personal psychological experiences, which are necessary for self-esteem regulation. Another way of describing these connections is by way of seeing them as sustaining empathic relationships. Such enduring relationships serve to maintain an integrated self.

Just as the one who is the target of sustained empathy is to be evaluated as to its ameliorative or negative aspects, so too must we consider the emotional impact on the so-called empathizer. It may be no easy task to persist in an empathic connection. Some time ago, I attended a case conference at which a severe schizophrenic patient was discussed in detail. One of the listeners spoke up to say that the material was simply too painful to stay with and so thereby illustrated the terrible state in which the patient lived. Empathy is always a two-way venture and may exert either a cost or a benefit to each participant. One is being asked to function as a particular selfobject when one enters into an empathic connection. Often this match is fortuitous, as when a patient asks to be mirrored and an analyst recognizes and responds as such. Sometimes the match is unworkable, as when a patient wishes to be mirrored and an analyst needs to be idealized. More important than the simple fitting together of a desired selfobject is the need to persist in the linkage over time. Once again, we must distinguish between a temporal slice of understanding and an enduring experience of sustained empathy.

PREREQUISITES FOR SUSTAINED EMPATHY

Thomas Metzinger (2009) is a philosopher and scientist who has suggested that we extend the concept of empathy to account for all of the different aspects of expressive behavior enabling us to establish a meaningful link with others. He proposed the term *shared manifold* to capture the phenomenological, functional, and subpersonal levels of human connection. The phenomenological is the conscious sense of similarity, the functional is the actions or emotions we observe in others, and the subpersonal is the activity of mirroring neural circuits. Similarly to most of those who liken empathy to something akin to textual reading, Metzinger assumed that we all read the same sentence and possibly interpret it differently. Similarly, in a recent column in a newspaper, the columnist listed a series of connections between the brain and psychology ranging from the situation of "menace" activating the amygdala, to the anterior cingulate mediating pain, and thereupon made a leap to how such studies may someday tell us "how people really are" (Brooks, 2009). These snapshots of human interaction construct a scenario in which the observer is outside of the inter-action. They fail to see that all empathy, both the immediate and the sustained, is a two-way street.

When we do observe as part of the interaction, we realize that a certain set of demands are placed upon the person practicing sus-tained empathy. The first of these demands is the requirement to avoid premature closure. This particular delay in decision making may require us to tolerate anxiety or any positive or negative effect associated with the particular memories and feelings aroused in us. Thus, for instance, the connection of so-called menacing with the amygdala might ordinarily stimulate our own functional aspect that Metzinger categorized, and so may lead us in a direc-tion that is not correlative to that of the person with whom we wish to be empathic. Indeed, there is no way that anyone can or should attempt to maintain a completely neutral position in sustaining one's empathy. Each category of Metzinger's should be calibrated in terms of the input of the empathizer. Thus, the second require-ment for sustained empathy is to understand and manage the fantasies that are stimulated in the person who is being empathic. These fantasies, of course, are valuable contributions to be con-sidered in the practice of empathy and are not to be dismissed or condemned but rather are to assist in understanding. If one is able to resist premature closure and to allow a recognition of one's personal contribution in this effort to understand another, then a third demand or requirement comes to the fore. This last needed activity is that of establishing one's own timeline and so breaking the empathic connection. This act of empathic disruption is said to be significant in terms of psychological growth and/or of possible insight. Much of that growth is predicated on the ability to reactivate an empathic connection that enables one to evaluate, again over time, the impact of sustained empathy followed by empathic disruption and its subsequent reconnection. Sustaining empathy is an act of careful and deliberate effort that imputes a responsibility to one that goes far beyond Metzinger's threefold levels. All observation imputes participation, and this participation varies from one observer to another.

MENTALIZATION

Mentalization is a somewhat newly popular term introduced to offer a theory of how mind reading is developed. It is said to be dependent on secure attachment (Fonagy, Gergely, Jurist, & Turget, 2002); types of attachment and attachment patterns in turn are said to be correlated with certain forms of pathology. Empathy is considered by some to be a form of mentalization (Firth & Wolpert, 2004, p. 115), and so *mentalization* joins a host of other words or phrases employed to make better sense of how people communicate with and understand others. At times, mentalization is restricted to observed behavior outside of language (Firth & Wolpert, 2004, p. 48), and at times an effort is made to explain it in a neuroscientific manner.

Mentalization is but one of a number of words and phrases that aim to differentiate a particular activity involved in a therapeutic relationship. Just as Basch (1983) preferred the phrase *empathic understanding*, others prefer *empathic immersion*, *attunement, empathic stance*, or similar variations on this single theme. The only distinction attributed to sustained empathy is that of the timeline that is required for determining the meaning that is formulated and the interpretation that is offered.

One can readily see how different psychoanalytic perspectives, each with its own terms and concepts, from interpersonal to intersubjective to relational, derive from the question asking,

"How does one person manage to determine what is going on in another person, and what is the impact of any and all such connections?" It is probably futile to attempt to differentiate these terms one from another, and it is likely that sustained empathy is a factor in them all. However, inasmuch as common or ordinary empathy is part and parcel of a host of psychological operations as well, it is important to carve out a particular activity that is the domain of sustained empathy. It is not mere listening. It is not mere mind reading. It is not merely having a relationship that is either interpersonal or intersubjective. It is all of these that lead to understanding over time,, and time is the crucial ingredient.

DISCUSSION

If we see sustained empathy as an ongoing fitting together of self-objects to aid in self-integration, we can extrapolate this form of connection from its role in psychoanalysis to all forms of social interactions. The selfobject transferences that arise in psychoanalysis result from a sustained empathic stance similar in type and form to those that emerge in all sorts of meaningful social relationships. Such enduring linkages differ in one crucial way in terms of effective treatment and something like mere group membership.

This difference is underlined by the analytic process, which aims to enable the person not to be independent of others but rather to form stable and sustainable empathic connections outside of the analytic situation. The analytic experience is not one to be copied or imitated outside of the consulting room but rather to be seen as enabling one to form sustaining empathic connections. It would be a fundamental error to see the loneliness of a person as treated by the companionship of a therapist or analyst, because loneliness is not a product of the lack of companionship as much as the inability to attain and retain companionship. To study isolation as an unfortunate situation, which it surely is, does not allow one to see how sustained empathy is an achievement and not a happenstance.

Empathy can be studied as a product of certain hormonal changes, as a particular form of brain activity, as a vital ingredient in the formation of social relationships, and even in its presence in animals from whales to nonhuman primates (deWaal, 2005). Inasmuch as these are different levels of inquiry, there is a danger that the term may be either trivialized to the point of losing its meaning or glorified to a point of a panacea for all sorts of problems.

In a somewhat abbreviated form, empathy is a method of data gathering (i.e., a category of mind reading). When we do read what we believe is going on in another person's mind, the data that we gather are regularly treated not so much as a bunch of words or sentences but rather as ideas laden with meaning. Empathy is thus not a mere registration of thoughts and feelings but is a complex configuration best thought of as a story or narrative. If we add the historical component to what we read in another's mind, we pursue empathy along a timeline and thus move to sustained empathy. This activity of gathering information about another often seems, in itself, to change the nature of the information that we gather. Not only does the observer affect the data gathered, but also the very act of observation changes both the observer along with the observed. Thus we conclude that some empathy is thought of as a single slice of information that is layered, and some as a lengthy set of information with a cause, a sequence, and a goal. It is suggested that the latter be separately categorized as sustained empathy and studied separately for its own therapeutic effects.

If one studies empathy primarily on the level of psychology, psychoanalytic self psychology offers a particular form of insight as to why it has both salutary and negative effects. The empathizer, or the one offering empathy, is experienced as a necessary self-object by the empathasand, or the one receiving the empathy. Over time, this meeting and matching of self and selfobject aid in self-integration and self-esteem regulation and so lead to a feeling of well-being. This feeling may, on occasion, well be shared by both participants. Thus, people feel better when understood and achieve an added feeling of self-cohesion when understood over time. Sustained empathy has a status that is qualitatively different than a short-term empathic connection with another person. Indeed, it may be one of the defining characteristics of human beings.

What becomes quite clear when a failed case is presented to a group of listeners is the struggle of these listeners to be empathic with the presenter along with being objective about the conduct of the case. Although no one might openly criticize the analyst or therapist, there were a number of whispered mutterings after the discussion was closed about how awful the treatment had been carried on and (often) how stupid this analyst or therapist had been. On occasion, there was a marked move to be supportive and even sympathetic to the presenter and so, inevitably, become dismissive or even negative about the patient. Failure often seems to do that to people, who abandon anything approaching a neutral position and either join with the patient in condemning the therapist or join with the therapist in an objectification of the patient, who is then seen more as a problem than as a person. These identifications, which are both natural and necessary, require a flexibility that most analysts and therapists are quite capable of attaining, but the need to relinquish the temporary status of the identifications is often lacking. We see, more often than not, a lasting impression that the patient was ill served by the failings of the treatment.

14

Rethinking Empathy

Just as many writers consider countertransference problems to be the core issue in failed cases, so too do others focus on failures in empathy as being central. Of course, it is convenient to have a single, central factor, but revisiting these supposed crucial points reveals their complexity and essential lack of readily belonging to a neat category. Especially with empathy, we can see how it is sometimes good and sometimes bad, sometimes easy to establish and sometimes impossible to achieve, and perhaps sometimes not particularly relevant.

A patient (someone who was unusually sensitive to the topic of empathy) recently told of an encounter with his roommate. The two had been sharing an apartment for several months, and one day the roommate asked that the temperature of the apartment be lowered or perhaps the heat be shut off entirely because "It is killing the planet." My patient responded that inasmuch as the thermostat was set at 68°F, and he felt comfortable at that setting, he was reluctant to lower it. He added that the point about the planet was, in his mind, pursuing the discussion at an irrelevant level of discourse. His roommate answered that this was a mere semantical difference. My patient said that all arguments were differences in semantics, and that they should discuss their different feelings sometime soon. As my patient recounted these events to me, he said he could well understand his roommate's position, and so he could probably agree to shutting off the heat and just wearing more clothes. He subsequently went around checking the thermostats at various friends' apartments and found none below 68°F, but he persisted in thinking it would be best to accede to his roommate's request.

When I asked my patient how he felt about this request, thinking of his probable subsequent discomfort, he said it was very difficult to think about his own feelings. My personal private thought, as one who enjoys a temperature of 70°F to 72°F, was that my patient surely must have been displeased if not enraged at this request of his roommate. As my patient struggled with an effort to recognize his own feelings, he said, "This is like empathy with a vengeance" (i.e., he seemed able to think only about "the other"). He then recalled (not for the first time) an incident with a bully in grade school that involved him being teased. He felt powerless in front of this bully. He soon told his mother about this unhappy situation, and then learned from her that his antagonist's parents were getting divorced, and so he was offered an explanation as a sort of justification for this bully's brutality. Armed with this information, the patient immediately confronted this bully with an aim to counter his teasing with his own weapon of retaliation, and so teased him about the divorce. My patient then announced to me that, in sharp distinction to his plight with his present roommate, he felt no empathy whatsoever toward this bully; he could concentrate only on his own feelings.

My patient continued to think about these two contrasting situations: thinking only of the other versus thinking only of himself. He shortly afterward experienced a change in his feelings both toward his roommate and toward his schoolyard foe. As to the first, he noted that he was angry at the (now) ridiculous request that all heat be turned off. He recognized that seeing the situation from what he felt was an empathic viewpoint seemed to blind him to both his own feelings and a (for him) "realistic" appraisal of the problem. As to the second, he realized that his own rage and helplessness at being bullied and finally being able to retaliate blinded him to his teaser's own torment at the breakup of his family. Now came the problem. He seemed able to feel either how his roommate must feel or how he felt toward his school bully. However, he also was able to understand how his tormenter came to his nasty disposition, just as he could understand how temperature meant so much to his roommate. Was this understanding that he had achieved a successful state of empathy toward these two? Or did he himself have to feel that he liked cold apartments and was equally entitled to mistreat and bully someone in the schoolyard?

Surely empathy need not be equivalent to full agreement—or should it? For a brief period, until he discussed it in treatment, he both agreed with his roommate and understood him. Yet once he recognized and felt his own position, which included his rage at the roommate, he no longer could feel the same as he had. Was he less empathic, no longer empathic, or what? Although he could understand the bully at school, he could neither agree with this cruelty nor feel any modicum of cruelty in himself. Had he managed to be empathic with the boy who was mean to him? When he talked about him in treatment, he felt less aggrieved at this mistreatment, but he never condoned it or, even for a moment, was able to give up his own feelings. Just as his original understanding of his roommate, with no concern for himself, was empathy with a vengeance or total empathy, so might his initial feelings about the bully qualify as an absence of empathy. There seemed to be no middle ground for him.

EMPATHY AND AGREEMENT

Empathy is defined by some as the natural capacity to share, appreciate, and respond to the affective state of others (Mason & Bartal, 2010). Of course, there are numerous different definitions and approaches to the word along with efforts to differentiate it from *sympathy* and *altruism*. It is necessarily an issue of semantics or a word with a fuzziness of meaning, but all natural languages contain ambiguity that is a feature that gives language its flexibility. Language needs its "flaws" in order to do the enormous range of things we use it for (Okrent, 2009). Thus, empathy can be considered as a transient identification, a vicarious introspection, "tasting but not swallowing," or a variety of other somewhat imprecise definitions. All of them involve taking up residence in another person's mind and thus unavoidably bringing along one's own baggage. If empathy involves anything approaching a full and lasting identification with another, then one is "overidentifying" and so is unable to attain a level of objectivity, much like my patient's initial perception and impression of his roommate. If one is totally unable to join with the other to experience an affective state, then a significant component of empathy is said to be lacking. Some amalgam of two psychic states is felt to be necessary, and so there exists the perhaps inevitable possibility of disagreement ("We two simply see the world differently"). These amalgams of personal feelings joined with shared elements of another's feeling are the necessary constituents of empathy, the middle ground.

A case mentioned in Chapter 11 was that of a middle-aged woman who had lost her husband and had entered analysis because of her prolonged bereavement. Shortly after entering into analysis, she joined a group of like-minded widows who shared a common belief that their deceased husbands were irreplaceable, and so it would be foolhardy to consider getting involved with another man. This patient had recurrent dreams that were characterized by the imagery of her sitting next to an empty chair. The analyst repeatedly interpreted the patient's resistance to getting involved with the analysis, but he soon felt that this was a futile exercise because of the patient's insistence that her lost husband was the "fine red wine that could not be replaced with Coca-Cola." Although there may be a number of commentaries and suggested approaches to this patient, these can be put aside to consider the comment from one of the members of the listening audience who claimed that the analyst was simply not empathic with his patient. His advice as to how to realize a state of empathic connection was to agree that her husband was indeed a perfect man, and that no other man could ever be as wonderful. This person indicated that it would not be enough for the analyst to simply state that he understood that his patient felt her late husband to be so irreplaceable; rather, the analyst must join her in this belief. The analyst took great exception to this advice and explanation, and said that although he could understand how she must feel, he could not agree with what was a fanciful and outrageous request. He balked at the idea that empathy demanded agreement. However, he could see that his patient felt that no one, save perhaps the members of her bereaved widows' association, could possibly understand her unless and until they agreed with her.

The analyst suggested a compromise. He could conjure up a relationship that he had had and had lost, and that he felt was irreplaceable. In this manner he could attain a similar feeling state that his patient had and so could share her affective state without sharing her belief. Would this qualify as empathy? Of course, the members of her widows' group went a step further and agreed with her belief, but this conviction eluded the analyst.

The discussion that (we may presume) followed aimed to tease apart sharing feelings, sharing beliefs, and (mere) understanding. Some felt all three features were necessary. Others settled for one or more. For *understanding*, there was agreement that it was essential but was another fuzzy term that could be seen as purely cognitive and therefore in need of a modifying adjective such as in the phrase *true or real understanding*. *Shared feeling* suffered a similar fate of insufficiency, inasmuch as it would appear to require an explanatory cognitive scaffold in order to fulfill the task of empathy. It seemed all too easy to feel with a patient without knowing the place of the feelings in the explanatory narrative. *Shared belief* was the most problematic. It was not clear if it was a universal requirement or one that was peculiar to some patients and not to others. Are there certain patients who need "understanding" to include agreement? That might be a solution of sorts; being empathic with any one patient may demand at times sharing feelings or at other times sharing beliefs; thus, *understanding* serves as a flexible term. There may well be easy cases and hard cases, and so next we move to the latter.

EMPATHY AND BEHAVIOR DISORDERS

People who behave in a way contrary to the usual mores of society test our empathic capacities and often strain them to a point that does not allow for success in understanding another. We recognize a common negative reaction to thieves, murderers, and scoundrels of all variety, and we rarely attempt to go beyond these reactions of abhorrence. There is an almost automatic reaction of anger toward those who misbehave, and although this sometimes evokes an interest in an effort to explain the behavior, rarely do we attain the level of concern attributed to empathy in which we "share, appreciate and respond to the affective state of others." Often we may decide that an offender is psychopathic or sociopathic, and thus we relegate him or her to a position that seems beyond psychology. We cannot join with such people in either an emotional or intellectual way no matter how interesting and intriguing they may be.

Recent studies of behavior disorders (Goldberg, 1999) have carved out a category of disorders characterized by parallel sectors of the psyche; one sector commits unacceptable behavior, and the other sector looks askance at and condemns it. These sectors are said to demonstrate a split in the psyche, and so psychological treatment is to be directed at this "vertical split." In these cases, the role of empathy is crucial. One may well be empathic with one sector, the one reflecting correct societal norms, and unempathic with the misbehaving one. All too commonly in these cases, the therapist joins with the patient in his or her dislike of misbehavior, and subsequent treatment becomes directed at various measures of control. Programs directed at controlling misbehavior, as in addictions, are representative of efforts to strengthen the socially acceptable sector in order to regulate and ultimately eliminate the misbehavior. In contrast to an effort at control is that of an empathic connection to the misbehaving sector, which is disavowed and split off. The struggle to attain a meaningful and lasting connection to an aspect of the psyche that is periodically offensive and even repulsive reawakens the question of whether empathy and agreement need go hand in hand.

The following cases are not presented as representative of correct technique, nor are they designed to argue the existence of this category of behavior disorders, both of which are discussed elsewhere (Goldberg, 2000). They are offered as a demonstration of the challenge of being empathic with this kind of patient. One may be carried along by the clinical material, but the majority of the histories and courses of treatment have been omitted in order to focus on how one feels about the patients who are presented.

CASE EXAMPLE

Dr. E. was a successful physician with a large and lucrative practice that he shared with a number of associates. Dr. E. enjoyed doing what he did as a physician and was respected and admired by his patients and colleagues. Dr. E., much to his recurrent periodic dismay, had secretive sexual relations with one or more of his complicit patients. Inasmuch as Dr. E. was married and the father of three children, he was constantly anxious lest he be discovered and exposed. Dr. E. went into psychotherapy because of both his unhappy marriage and his anxiety about involving his many patients in sexual activity. The sexual relations with his patients were not very long lasting and were usually erratic and very unpredictable. He insisted that he was never in love with any of these patients, save for one with whom he entertained ideas of divorcing his wife and marrying her. He said he enjoyed the relationships as much as the sex. Although Dr. E. had no hesitation in claiming that what he did was stupid, he also felt that every man wished to do the same; the fear of getting caught dissuaded them. His characterization of his behavior as "stupid" did not extend to its also being labeled as bad or sinful or wrong. It was just dumb.

Dr. E's therapist was careful not to condemn or criticize him for his dalliances with his patients but rather concentrated on his unhappy marriage and the chance of his getting into trouble for what he did. As Dr. E. disregarded the advice of his therapist, the therapist decided that he was at his wit's end and referred him to another therapist. This initial therapist felt that Dr. E. was doing something wrong; he could hardly agree that this type of behavior was merely stupid. Interestingly, one of Dr. E's partners also was unfaithful to his wife but extended his sexual activity to both patients and hospital personnel. Together, they shared a secret pleasure in their misbehavior and supported one another.

Suddenly, while in his new therapy, Dr. E. was confronted with the possible exposure of his misbehavior by one of his patients; he felt that his first therapist's warnings were prophetic, and swore that he would never again take such a risk. However, his resolve was short-lived, and once again he began to look for opportunities. Dr. E. wanted his therapist to join with him in recognizing the need for these "perfectly harmless" escapades, which were never to be thought of as his taking advantage of anyone. This second therapist realized that in order to be empathic with his new patient, he would have to agree with the tenet that this activity was indeed stupid rather than evil. Dr. E. had no trouble in recognizing the disapproval of his first therapist and registering such disapproval as his being misunderstood. Of course, Dr. E. would not argue with anyone who felt that he was doing wrong. He just did not agree with them. Dr. E's second therapist realized that Dr. E. required agreement to fulfill the achievement of an empathic connection. Although Dr. E. felt that he did things that he later regretted and wished that he had not succumbed to these temptations, he also rationalized his behavior as something that he deserved, because he and his wife no longer enjoyed sexual relations; they were usually cool to and distant from one another. No matter how one might conceptualize Dr. E's psychic organization, or what one might consider an effective treatment of Dr. E., he did feel that in order to understand him, one had to see things the way he did.

A somewhat dramatic contrast to the case of Dr. E. is that of John, which I reported in another publication (Goldberg, 1995).

CASE EXAMPLE

John also was a physician who was involved in sexual relations with his patients. For John, they were but anonymous vehicles for performing oral fellatio. John had a ritualized sexual encounter with his patients that occurred randomly and episodically, and was always followed by profound feelings that were only later in his analysis characterized as shame and remorse. John felt terrible about what he did, resolved never to do it again, yet regularly found himself engaged in the same sort of sexual activity. In his first analysis, John was advised to masturbate before seeing his patients in order to diminish the chances of his acting out. Once again, misbehavior was seen as something to be controlled, regulated, and eradicated. It was not difficult for the second analyst to become empathic with the symbolism of these sexual escapades, and so to join with John in seeing them as not only shameful but also in need of being understood.

The contrast between Dr. E. and John may be seen by some as significant and by others as insignificant. Once again, these cases are not presented as exercises in diagnosis and/or treatment but rather as empathic challenges. Whereas John felt that what he did was wrong, shameful, and something he wished to disown, Dr. E. felt his behavior was stupid, wrong, and something he only periodically wanted to disown. However, John did not feel that his behavior was wrong during its commission, but only in retrospect. In that respect, he was not unlike Dr. E., who enjoyed his sexual activity and knew that it was wrong according to society's standards. Dr. E differed from John primarily in the subsequent feelings of shame.

If we concentrate on a therapist's efforts to understand these men, there is little doubt that they evoke different feelings and therefore different challenges. The developmental history of John evokes more sympathy, and the ritualized activity that he participated in invites more curiosity about its meaning. Although the developmental history of Dr. E. may also evoke a sympathetic approach, this quickly evaporates as he justifies his misbehavior with rationalizations of deserving some pleasure. John and Dr. E. also differ in their relationships with their patients, who are basically unknown; they remain so to John, whereas Dr. E. insists that getting to know them better is as important as the sex. Both John and Dr. E. initially had therapists who were upset by their symptoms and wished to control them in some way. Only later did each have a therapist who felt that understanding their symptoms was the best road to their possible removal. However, understanding was quite different for each man.

UNDERSTANDING AS MULTIDIMENSIONAL

The three essential components that were listed previously as comprising empathy are sharing feelings, appreciating feelings, and responding to feelings. Together they add up to understanding. The first of the triad seems easiest, although we saw with my patient and his roommate and his history of being bullied that the sharing of feelings that is never sufficient, always requires some effort, and is modified as one brings one's own prejudices to bear. The second, appreciating feelings, brings forth one's own evaluation and ultimate acceptance or rejection of the feelings. One can overidentify with or, by contrast, condemn the patient. This is where the issue of agreeing with the patient seems paramount, and where the question of morality often rears its head. One can appreciate why someone feels a certain way, but one cannot necessarily condone it. Many people, however, feel that they are not really understood until and unless their feelings are condoned. And, like it or not, many people cannot be helped unless and until they feel so understood. Indeed, the very act of sharing feelings often requires an agreement as to the legitimacy of the feelings. The triad of the components of empathy may be so intertwined in some people that they cannot be individually considered.

DISCUSSION

Some authors (e.g., deWaal, 2005) have differentiated *empathy*, the ability to understand another situation, from *empathic concern*, which has the added feature of caring and therefore can promote good or bad. There are usually a number of such distinctions and qualifications to the term as it is extended to words such as *sympathy* and *altruism*, as it is studied in nonhuman primates, and as its biochemical substrate is investigated. When we focus on its use in psychoanalysis and dynamic psychology, it is best thought of in its basic therapeutic function. Here it is commonly seen as a sustained effort to understand another in depth, and it is recognized as often having a therapeutic effect in its own right. Like Humpty Dumpty in *Through the Looking Glass*, empathy means exactly what the person employing it wishes it to mean.

One can establish a linear series of the ways empathy is thought of. It ranges from the spreading of a yawn throughout a group of chimps or humans (Mason & Bartal, 2010, p. 2), on to the purely cognitive capacity to perceive another's emotional state even if quite different from one's own, to the empathic triad of sharing beliefs, appreciating beliefs, and responding to these beliefs. And of course, the last can be considered in either a positive caring manner or a negative destructive one.

Restricting the consideration of empathy to its role in psychoanalytic thinking allows or insists that we recognize that naïve statements such as "Empathy is an invisible force whose presence brings out our best and whose absence, or indeed abuse, permits atrocities" (Mason & Bartal, 2010, p. 1) are oversimplified misunderstandings. Rather, empathy is better thought of as a particular form of data gathering or investigation of others that, although it may be positive or negative in its intention, affects people differently. Therefore, another linear series extends from the mere perception of another to the complex sharing of feelings and beliefs of another. Empathy in this series impacts people differently. Some people may feel better or may feel worse in being understood. Some feel better having shared their feelings, whereas some require that they have their feelings and beliefs shared, acknowledged, and agreed with. This last is most important in a therapeutic endeavor because it often delineates the extent of our capacity to be empathic.

The morning paper reports the trial of a man who kidnapped and raped a young girl whom he kept captive for many years and repeatedly abused (*New York Times*, March 20, 2010, p. A9). It also details some of the forms of sexual molestation he visited upon his victim. Most readers would readily share feelings with the unfortunate little girl but could not do so with the offender. Most therapists could not treat him, because they could not extend their empathy to fully understand him. Both victim and offender demonstrate the range of the targets of our empathy. But both also illustrate the limits of our therapeutic capacities. It is relatively easy to feel for someone who is mistreated, and it is enormously difficult to do so for a scoundrel who hurts others. However, in a therapeutic sense they both require empathy and perhaps sometimes even an agreement with their feelings.

The complexity and range of the concept of empathy in psychoanalysis and dynamic psychotherapy require recognition not only of its different usages but also of the fact that it affects different people differently. Therefore, empathy must be seen in two perspectives: the capacity and limitations of the person extending empathy, and the impact on the person who is the target of the empathy. Just as we are all not capable of understanding everyone, so, too, are we all affected differently by attempts to understand us. The most common misconception in the world of therapy is its concern and emphasis on being empathic with others, assuming everyone reacts similarly and that the reaction is a positive one. Persons who wish to take advantage of others and/or to hurt them may well be exquisitely empathic. So, too, may some whom we may wish to help but who will not allow us entry into their inner world. The two-way street of empathy demands our continued resistance to reductionism or oversimplification. With the newly awakened interest in empathy created by the study of mirror neurons and the application of the concept to nonhuman primates, it is more critical than ever for psychoanalysis to clarify what the word means for the discipline.

15

Self Psychology and Failure

Despite the varieties of failed cases noted and described in this book, and therefore in no way indicating that there is a single cause for failure, there are both cases that best exemplify a clear cause and those that best explain why so many analysts and therapists have been reluctant to present and discuss failed cases. That these cases are best explained using the theory offered by self psychology is either the author's preference or the truth.

The concept of idealization is a fairly well-established basic tenet in today's psychoanalytic thinking with its normal development underscoring the child's imbuing his or her parents with the powers to fix everything and to make the world a safe and happy place. So, too, does normal development allow for a gradual and nontraumatic diminishment of this idealization as the child recognizes parental limitations and thereby likewise assumes the job of fixing things and making the world a safe and happy place for himself or herself. This process of recognizing what may be called the *realistic appraisal of the "ideal" parent* is considered to be carried out over time, and it is defined as being nontraumatic if it carries just enough of the affect of disappointment to be manageable, tolerable, and relatively free of rage. Of course, this optimal course of what is essentially a process of phase-specific disillusionment is fraught with moments of potential trauma for the developing child. This is frequently coupled with the reluctance of one or both parents to manage his or her feelings as failing to live up to any and all expectations that are seen as reflecting of personal inadequacies, ones that cannot be easily acknowledged.

There are many derivatives of the process of idealization and deidealization, and these range from pseudo-idealization, which carries an element of mockery and may be seen in the overvaluing of the unworthy, on to the forms of pathology associated with traumatic deidealization. The following is an illustration of the latter.

CASE EXAMPLE

Stephen was visiting a new social worker after a disappointing series of encounters with a number of psychotherapists. This particular psychotherapist seemed to be more caring and interested in Stephen, and so the treatment appeared to be more promising than others. Stephen's life was a sad one in that he had been taken from his mother when he was but 2 years of age after his estranged father discovered that his infant son was left without food or clean diapers for extended periods of time. The father arranged for Stephen to be adopted by his own parents, who were quite well off and more than eager to adopt Stephen. Years went by before Stephen saw his mother again, this time in a mental hospital with her hardly recognizing or remembering him.

Stephen's upbringing by these wealthy grandparents was not particularly smooth inasmuch as he became the designated heir to a large amount of money and so became surrounded by what he described as a host of jealous relatives. Money was a central issue in this new therapy, and the psychotherapist social worker was quick to realize this, as well as to recognize his own valuation of the desirable patient whom he claimed to be genuinely fond of.

Stephen often complained to his therapist of both anxiety and insomnia, and repeatedly asked to be referred to a psychiatrist for medication. In reporting the case to a supervisor, the therapist admitted to being slow to respond to Stephen's requests, but at long last did make a referral to someone who he did not personally know but had only heard about from a colleague. The appointment with this physician was noteworthy in that Stephen was told that he needed medication, and that his social worker therapist was dilatory in attending to this. Stephen reported this information to his therapist, who could only agree and apologize for his deficiency. The supervisor of the case asked the therapist how he felt about his not being able or knowledgeable enough to prescribe, and this therapist insisted that such thoughts and ambitions had never entered his mind. When pressed as to how Stephen might have felt about this particular area of deficiency, inadequacy, or limitation of his therapist, the answer was one that reported a series of angry and violent thoughts that Stephen was having about this therapist.

We might assume that the supposed failure of Stephen's therapist to properly care for him echoed the failure of his mother to do the same when he was a small child. The subsequent "adoption" of failure by his therapist allowed that word to carry the multiple meanings of adoption ascribed to Stephen's childhood. Rather than interpret the rage that Stephen was experiencing and that so characterizes traumatic deidealization, this therapist allowed himself to be the living embodiment of failure. His own countertransferences seemed to prevent him from allowing himself to experience his own anger at the position he found himself in with his own limitations as a social worker clinician who cannot prescribe as well as at the initial psychiatrist, who chose to visit his personal struggle with his own significance upon this hapless therapist.

Patients who suffered a sudden and often inexplainable disruption in their relationship to a parental ideal regularly respond with rage and a continuing fragility of the self. The latter often takes the form of poor self-regulation and an easily disordered self-integration. Psychotherapists may see this sort of a patient as a sorrowful soul, and on occasion may choose to adopt a stance that in some manner aims to compensate the patient for the trauma that he or she has suffered. Once embarked on this road, it may be difficult to determine acceptable and tolerable boundaries of this compensatory effort. From the totally unavailable parent to the parent who cannot tolerate normal and expectable limitations of parenting, we see the range of disappointments seen by the child and predictably assigned to the parent who has failed. Too often, the therapist who wishes to do too much misses the recognition and interpretation of the inevitable failure.

AN OPERATING THEORY

In an interesting footnote in *The Restoration of the Self* (1977, p. 173), Heinz Kohut compared the classical Freudian method by which an analyst learns about a patient's childhood to his own method. He stated that Freud felt that clinical transferences were repetitions of childhood experiences, whereas self psychology noted the reactivation of thwarted attempts at structure building. Thus, the selfobject transferences are a new edition of the relation between the self and its selfobjects. It allows development to resume.

Although possibly subject to a variety of interpretations, this footnote does seem to indicate that a new developmental experience can take place in an analysis or a psychotherapy as opposed to a mere emotional reliving of a traumatic experience with an ensuing redeployment of drives and an acceptance of one's personal history. The misinterpretations of this footnote extend from treatment becoming a form of reparenting to all varieties of therapy as reparations for the suffering that was endured. If, indeed, one is to serve as some sort of scaffolding or presence for self-development to resume, does this not imply that the therapist must "be something"? Mere reexperiencing of the rage and disappointment that may have characterized one's childhood surely cannot by itself be reparative. Must one not also make it up to the patient? Knowing that you are hungry does not fill one's stomach. One must distinguish between recognizing the rage, apologizing for the failure that led to the rage, and compensating for that same failure by an act of perhaps crossing a boundary (i.e., acting like a better parent).

In an excellent review of what characterizes the opposing views of the self psychological process of analysis, Gehrie (2009) compared the idea of "optimal frustration" to that of "optimal gratification" and likened the latter to the variety of "relational" techniques that have been developed and popularized as forms of analytic therapy. He felt that "the relational emphasis does not permit a full exploration of the unconscious, split-off dimensions of archaic (and often negatively charged) self-states caused by the emphasis on provision in the here-and-now of the relationship" (p. 47). As such, Gehrie felt optimal gratification leads to forms of idealizations of the analyst that tend not to be subsequently analyzed (p. 39). Although the analysis of idealization has been extensively discussed by Kohut (1971, pp. 2–37), the emphasis to be focused on here has to do with early traumatic deidealization, and so no attempt will be made to review that process best explained by Kohut.

NONTRAUMATIC DEIDEALIZATION

The omnipotence and omniscience assigned to the parent initially give comfort and the feeling of safety to the child and lend the experience of dependability and reliability to the emerging self. The self becomes strengthened and better integrated by way of its reliance and connection to the idealized other. It is said that the first undetected lie reveals to the child that the parent is not omnipotent and cannot read the child's mind, and so allows for a beginning disillusionment with the parent along with a feeling of pride and mastery to the child (Kohut, 1984, pp. 71–72). The ensuing moments of disappointment and recognition of parental limitations do not by any means lead to a break with the parent but allow an internalization of the parent in the form of appropriate goals and aims. Kohut concluded that the phase-appropriate internalizations built up two permanent core structures of the personality: the neutralizing basic fabric of the psyche, and the idealized superego (Kohut, 1977, p. 40). Elsewhere I wrote that the child's relationship to the parental ideal results in the inner feelings of predictability, dependability, and reliability (Goldberg, 1988, p. 68). Failures in the gradual internalizing process lead to diffuse narcissistic vulnerability and a never-ending search for the archaic idealized other.

TRAUMATIC DEIDEALIZATION

In order to solve the question as to whether insight or reparenting solves the problem of insufficient and defective development of idealization, another clinical example is in order.

CASE EXAMPLE

Lydia was, like Stephen, a much-neglected and uncared-for child whose mother was a chronic alcoholic and whose father was said to be passive and unable or unwilling to do much about assuring proper care for his daughter. Also like Stephen, Lydia had a rather colorful and disordered psychiatric history, which included both multiple diagnoses along with some prolonged periods of hospitalization. Lydia never seemed able to carve out a career for herself or a settled domestic life in that she never married or held a job. Her major contacts in life were a variety of service men or women who cared for her needs ranging from shopping to driving to gardening. However, Lydia also used the services of mental health professionals from psychologists to psychopharmacologists. She was usually unhappy and dissatisfied with the quality of these services, but one day Lydia discovered a psychiatrist who seemed especially interested in and even devoted to her. This therapist saw Lydia whenever she wished, allowed her to call as often as she felt the need, and even rescheduled a vacation to be available to Lydia. The availability of this therapist both pleased and puzzled

Lydia, but in the main she took full advantage of the situation and felt close to and cared for by this therapist. However, dissatisfaction began to appear as Lydia became angry over the fact that despite this rather intense form of treatment, she remained without a husband or a career. She became more and more enraged at this therapist, who was unable to fully explain Lydia's lack of fulfillment to her. Finally, Lydia quit this therapist as she had done to so many others, and began working with a new therapist who quickly set limits on Lydia's treatment by banning all phone calls and setting a strict schedule.

This new therapist in rather short order noted a pattern in Lydia's life of recurrent disappointment followed by intense rage and despair. Lydia would shop long and hard for a perfect outfit, consult at length with the salesperson until she found exactly what she wanted, and have it delivered only to discover that it was all wrong. Not only would Lydia have to return the outfit, but also her anger at the salesperson would further ruin the experience. When this new therapist decided to offer her newfound understanding and interpretation to Lydia, she waited until Lydia had recounted her most recent shopping disaster before telling Lydia of her insight. No sooner had she finished her explanation than Lydia announced that she could see that the therapist had been waiting while she talked on and on just to say what she had on her mind. She wasn't really listening. And no matter if what she said was true or not, she had not done a very good job of delivering it. And so this new promising therapist joined the ranks of those who had failed Lydia.

The therapists of both Stephen and Lydia felt themselves failures. The first had apologized for his failings, and the second was the recipient of a rageful outburst. Whereas Lydia's first therapist tried mightily to be as good and caring as possible in order to help heal this patient's legitimate feelings of neglect, and the second felt that limit setting and explanation might do the trick, neither seemed particularly effective. Stephen and Lydia had each endured early trauma for which insight and/or compensation appeared to be fruitless. Indeed, it was likely that the developmental trauma endured by these patients was a preverbal one, and so was not immediately subject to verbal processing. Lydia's first therapist was involved in a series of actions to facilitate a feeling of being cared for in Lydia. Stephen needed both medication and an admission of being wronged, but neither seemed of lasting benefit. Each therapist struggled with thwarted hope and inevitable failure.

To return to the footnote that distinguishes the benefit attributed to childhood recall from that dependent on a reawakened development, we may be able to craft a proper technique that neither compensates in the manner of optimal gratification nor interprets what has been newly remembered. The essential point of optimal frustration lies in the fact of the disappointment being real, tolerable, and structure building. Thus the therapist must recognize that he or she has failed without apology or denial but with an effort to discuss, to bring into words the associated anger. Just as the first undetected lie allows a continued connection to the fallible parent with a subsequent internalization and identification with the parental ideal, so too must the developmental process be reactivated and resumed with the fallible therapist. To put it in a rather painful nutshell: The analyst or therapist must acknowledge the failure, not apologize for the failure, not make amends for the failure, not attempt to explain the failure away, but rather allow the failure to be. Only then can it be interpreted in terms of a childhood that was fraught with both unmanageable and undiscussed or unacknowledged failure.

Too often, the inevitable failures that occur in psychotherapy or psychoanalysis become subjects of blame or responsibility and thereby difficult to be seen as necessary and even desirable. The need to investigate and analyze failure is directed at its undoing rather than its welcome. To see failure as an expectable moment in treatment often means that the nature of or the responsibility for the failure is fundamentally irrelevant. Often, the analysis of failure is aimed at absolution and so removes it from the developmental process.

DISCUSSION

Psychoanalysts and psychotherapists make lots of mistakes. They sometimes start late or end early or overcharge or undercharge. They say the wrong thing or do not say the right thing. Often, they apologize or explain. Sometimes, they deny or defend themselves. Perhaps more often, they discuss and interpret and analyze the errors with benefit. However, there are patients who essentially need the therapist or analyst to be wrong, to realize that they are wrong, and to recognize what that experience of a failed ideal means. Corresponding to the need to evoke a feeling of failure in a therapist is the extreme discomfort of therapists who feel they have failed. It is important to note that patients do not necessarily wish the treatment as a whole to be a failure but rather to have the therapist or analyst to be a failure. This, again, should not be read as an effort to defeat the treatment but as an indicator of a meaningful childhood experience of the patient that must be communicated to the therapist. Those traumatic failures that occurred preverbally must, not surprisingly, be situations of actions rather than of words.

As much as a patient who has experienced an early traumatic deidealization needs to create or recreate a replica of that experience in the treatment, he or she also wishes to resume a corrective development. The biggest hurdle to the sought-for "reactivation of a thwarted attempt at structure building" (Kohut, 1977, p. 173) is the countertransference of the analyst or therapist who cannot tolerate being wrong. The rescue fantasies that fuel the profession are deterrences to the analysis of traumatic deidealization. The rage of the disillusioned patient leads to a natural reaction of guilt, which stimulates a variety of responses ranging from a wish to make amends, to reactive anger at being accused, to outright denial of wrongdoing. It is difficult to be neutral about being incompetent.

In support of the position that decries "optimal gratification," it should be clear that any activity that offers apologies or compensation for the wrongdoing of the therapist is an obstacle to the analysis of the error that, perhaps paradoxically, was a needed error. The developmental process proceeds by the phase-specific nontraumatic failures and not by any form of appeasement or gratification as a result of the mistakes that must occur.

THE PROCESS

The essence of a so-called reparenting experience or a corrective emotional experience is that of offering a patient a relationship that is significantly different from that of a childhood that is felt to be responsible for adult pathology. The new and corrective experience is said to ameliorate the trauma of yesteryear. The essence of a classical analysis is the appearance of transferences that are repetitions of childhood experience, and the insight that results from these repetitions leads to a mastery of the adult pathology. The modification of this classical position by self psychology is that of creating an atmosphere for the resumption of self-development.

The reactivation of the process of development requires no specific technical activity inasmuch as the very act of interpretation involves the sequence of an empathic connection followed by an empathic break or disruption (Kohut, 1984, p. 172). This sequence is representative of a structure-building internalization as the patient assumes the position of self-understanding, a position that is relinquished by the analyst or therapist. In this manner, the classical Freudian position that was championed by Gitelson is allowed to maintain its basic technical operation while being expanded by Kohut's self-psychological insights. The move from traumatic deidealization to the phase-specific nontraumatic deidealization can, of course, be seen as corrective but no more than sustained empathy and insight likewise are components of the therapeutic process.

Some of the failed experiences in psychotherapy and psychoanalysis must be seen as necessary reenactments of childhood experiences, as transference phenomena of self-object failures.

Too often, the countertransference positions that demand an acknowledgment and acceptance of these transference configurations are resisted by therapists in the form of a denial, an apology, or perhaps compensation. These responses are subsequently rationalized in one or another form of theoretical modifications, and their analysis is waylaid in order to sustain a rescue fantasy and to avoid the discomfort of failure. Negative transference configurations are often elaborations of what may be considered to be minor mistakes and therefore easily lend themselves to reality debates and discussions in order to dissipate this discomfort. This may be explained by a theoretical need for a relationship or some form of interaction, thus again to avoid the therapist's acceptance of failure. Only the latter opens the door to a proper analytic investigation of failure based upon early traumatic deidealization.

16

The Future for Failure

One inescapable fact that becomes quickly apparent in any study of failure is that the major problems are concentrated at both ends: Many patients fail to start any form of meaningful treatment, just as many patients are ultimately tagged as untreatable. As noted in chapters throughout this book, the dropout rate can be as high as 67.3% in some forms of therapy, but a comparable statistic is not available for untreatability because so much depends on the particular form of therapy being considered. We noted in an earlier chapter that some analysts have suggested that all patients be considered for analysis with no prior judgment as to suitability. The same may well be true for other forms of treatment.

In terms of patients who never really start any therapy, the comparison to the number of patients who receive prescriptions for medication that are not filled or those who fill the prescriptions but fail to take the medication is a starkly similar problem. There are a number of anecdotal explanations for these lapses, ranging from "I felt better without doing anything" to "I just did not trust that doctor," that may cover this phenomenon, but no one has conducted a large-scale study that goes beyond these anecdotes. It is true that the placebo effect accounts for a good deal of these magical improvements, and no doubt some immediate transference reactions might well explain others. Money is always a significant factor because one can markedly reduce dropout rates by eliminating fees. This, of course, flies in the face of the many therapeutic rationalizations for charging fees. All in all, however, it cannot be denied that many patients who might benefit from psychotherapy or psychoanalysis are not availing themselves of these benefits for reasons ranging from unavailability to unaffordability to diverse psychological factors. It is to the latter that more attention should be paid. Once again, there is much anecdotal evidence that some potential patients are more likely to seek out priests, ministers, or rabbis than psychotherapists or psychoanalysts, and a class of therapists who are also religiously trained has developed to meet this need. Yet the bulk of untreated patients remains unstudied and of little concern.

A close corollary to the category of potential patients who remain outside of any form of psychological intervention is the group who have been earlier discussed: those who in some manner or other break off treatment. Vagueness dominates the scene as one attempts to determine if a treatment consisting of a few sessions can qualify as a bona fide course of treatment or if an attempt to distinguish short-term treatment from long-term treatment can serve as a guide to decide just when treatment is to be considered broken off. A surprisingly large number of cases in psychoanalysis seem to fit into this category (i.e., "The patient just quit"). A study of long-term psychotherapy reported that the duration of treatment was not a significant factor in patient improvement, but the number of sessions was (Leichsenring & Robung, 2008). Again, these statistics allow for a variety of guesswork as to reasonable explanations, but there is not much research about why patients drop out, discontinue, or fail to benefit from either psychodynamic psychotherapy or psychoanalysis. In contrast to this paucity of information, not surprisingly more and more research is being done on the efficacy of long-term psychotherapy (Leichsenring & Robung, 2008) as well as the cost-effectiveness of all forms of therapy (Lazar, 2010) and the enduring effects of psychoanalysis (Kantrowitz, 1996). However, this is a brief for a proper study of failure. Like the runt of the litter, failure in truth requires more rather than less attention. As I hope to have shown, its neglect is a product of our own denial and shortcomings, and the rewards of greater attention may surprise us, or at least we hope so.

At the other end of the spectrum of failed cases that fail to start are the accumulated versions of cases that are more or less discarded as untreatable. To further pursue the quaint linguistic phraseology of our psychiatric brethren, we may assume the following: If a particular form of treatment helps or cures one or more patients who suffer from a circumscribed mental problem, then the application of that same treatment, no matter when it is applied, to another patient, and the failure of that treatment on this subsequent patient, would then qualify this less fortunate patient to be labeled as *treatment resistant*. Of course, only the failure of every conceivable treatment would allow one to say that the patient is "resistant" to treatment.

The story seems much different, and the vocabulary wholly different, when it comes to psychotherapy and psychoanalysis. The latter allows for patients who are unanalyzable as well as those who are successfully analyzed without much of an observable change to be lumped together with failed cases as outwardly unchanged. Each and every one of these points about what is alterable and what not is arguably and desperately in need of further study. As long as the present state of affairs claims that every patient should be analyzed until we can identify the "moderators" that allow for successful treatment, then analysis would seem to be unable to differentiate those patients who cannot get started from those who break off an analysis before a successful termination, from those who are successfully analyzed with no diminution in symptomatology, and from those who are successfully analyzed. However, not only the vocabulary but also the responsibility for results differ between psychiatry and psychoanalysis. Many analysts consider each of the above temporal considerations—from starting to interrupting to terminating—to depend on the analyst, because of a good or bad "match," a competent or incompetent practitioner, or an unwise theoretical approach. Lurking in the background are the extremes: from "It is no one's fault that the patient did not get better" in psychiatry to the equally problematic "It is all my fault" on the part of the psychoanalyst.

Whether or not psychotherapy is much different from psychoanalysis in its approach to untreatability is filled with qualifications. These qualifications are similar to those that are seen in psychoanalysis and essentially apply to an oft-noted issue in this book: Treatability or untreatability depends on the applicability of the form of treatment to the pathology of the patient. Recent work on the psychotherapy of patients diagnosed as having borderline personality disorders (Kernberg, 1999) points the way to our being more definitive in the utilization of certain techniques to particular forms of pathology. This is also seen in some arenas of psychoanalysis in the treatment of behavior disorders (Goldberg, 2000). Of course, claims have always been raised as to the effectiveness of one theory or technique of analysis or therapy, but we lack the specificity that may be seen (say) in the treatment of borderline disorders by a specific form of psychodynamic intervention. The ultimate goal should be one that directs efforts to determine more closely what treatment works best for what disorders. The combined efforts of many practitioners to elaborate diagnostic categories based upon observable phenomena, such as in the construction of a diagnostic manual, might well be better served in the pursuit of a closer tie between pathology and therapy.

Perhaps nowhere in the field of psychological treatment is untreatability more painfully obvious than in the study of suicide, and nowhere is the result more in need of study than in successful suicide. I once attended a conference where the staff of a hospital unit devoted to suicidal patients presented their fundamental belief that only a persistent and oft-repeated message to their patients of "We do not want you to kill yourself" was effective. They felt that this communication neutralized the message of others in the patient's life that indicated exactly the opposite. I do not know the statistics of their success rate, but their mantra might reveal a common countertransference problems of many therapists and analysts that we have discussed (in Chapter 13), including those who deal with suicide: the patient's wish to make one feel a failure and the reactive struggle to prove oneself a success. This mimics the painful deidealization that so many parents cannot endure; it is regularly acted out, as in the conference I attended, rather than interpreted. When the forlorn parents of a suicide victim are reassured by the psychiatrist, psychotherapist, or psychoanalyst, "Everything was done, and no one is to blame," they are sometimes unable to adequately reckon with the feeling of failure that the patient was trying to have the parent realize and acknowledge. Perhaps embracing failure will ultimately lead to understanding it. As awkward as the idea may seem, the definition of failure is not merely the opposite of success. Sometimes it is inevitable. Sometimes it is warranted. It always needs to be confronted.

To think of failure in what may be an unusual or perhaps perverse fashion, one might ask, "What are the circumstances that would allow it to flourish?" Failure develops best in those unflexible and fixed environments that are slow or reluctant to adapt. This rigidity can be evidenced in areas of application such as time or frequency as well as method. Some patients may need longer or shorter encounters with a therapist or in the applications of a particular procedure. Some should be seen four times a week, and some only once per month. It is important that one recognize that alterations in frequency not be seen merely or primarily as deviations from a correct procedure, because the very introduction of the idea of a deviation begins to mark the treatment as being out of the ordinary rather than what best fits a particular patient. The ability of a therapist to both recognize and realize the patient's needs should not be seen as either a limitation or a countertransference problem but more as an illustration of a "proper match," as Kantrowitz (1995) has noted. However, the match goes beyond the personal attributes of the therapist or analyst to the particular schools of thought such as Kleinian or Kohutian as well as to the use of cognitive-behavioral therapy (CBT) or medication. Allegiances to unvarying belief systems are fertile grounds for failure.

Another arena for the probability of a failure is that of ambition, both of the therapist and of the patient. Just as we have noted that despair can become the undoing of a suicidal patient, so can hope become the ruination of an overeager patient or therapist. Our rescue fantasies both fuel our efforts and blind us to realistic limitations. Failure thrives in an atmosphere of heightened expectations. Perhaps the overidealization of psychoanalysis, which once was considered as "something that you should do if you could," is a good example of a treatment that may not be in the best interests of a patient. What an analyst or therapist feels is best may not be best for a given patient. We sometimes hear the following: "Ideally this patient should be seen four times a week for several years." The employment of the word *ideally* betrays what may be a misplaced ambition rather than a careful appraisal of the patient's needs. It is often difficult to tear one's self away from an internal rating system of good, better, and best therapies without registering a sense of disappointment that becomes evident to a patient.

The timing of treatment is also a paramount factor in its ultimate failure. We regularly determine the best form of therapy or analysis for a patient at the wrong time, inasmuch as it is difficult to have all of the ingredients of patient, therapist, and form of treatment come together at a propitious time. Lacking that crucial component, treatment may be urged or even forced at what ultimately turns out to be the wrong time. Sadly, this particular mishap is only (if ever) recognized in retrospect. Fortunately, another effort with similar components may be successful at another time. There is something to be said for a patient as well as a therapist or analyst to be "ready," and it is often the case that our personal desire to begin clouds our perception of such readiness.

There are doubtless other aspects of an analysis or psychotherapy that are significant issues to be considered in a likely or predestined failure, but the last to be offered to be thought about here is the awareness of the patient's larger ecosystem including family, friends, social class, and so on. We are all aware of the "ripple" effect of psychotherapy or psychoanalysis, and we often appreciate the fact that a positive change in a patient has an associated positive effect on those around him or her. The opposition to the ripple effect is composed of the panoply of forces that resist change and so will not allow an analysis or therapy to proceed. The tendency to concentrate diagnosis and prognosis on the assets and liabilities of the patient for a desirable endpoint often lead one to ignore or neglect the forces that promote failure. Recognition of a more or less stable system that will resist disruption is a necessity as any treatment is undertaken. Whenever the status quo is threatened, there may be a corresponding counterreaction to the threat. Sometimes the need for the treatment to fail may come from an unlikely source that was initially quite supportive of the treatment.

Inasmuch as failure may be thought of as the flip side of success, they both can be seen as sharing the same elements or components to enable reaching their eventual endpoints. For example, support or discouragement from a spouse, symptom relief versus secondary gain, or any number of binary oppositions must be reckoned with in an analysis of success and failure. The tendency to ignore or deny the likelihood of failure is the greatest boon to its eventual emergence. If it is seen as an equal partner to success, it may enter the light of day and so become available for further scrutiny and analysis.

The same sort of encouragement or sabotage that we may find in the family or support system of potential patients is also seen in the field of psychotherapy and psychoanalysis and in their collection of schools and theories. Just as psychopharmacologists delight in medicating patients who have not done well in psychoanalysis and psychoanalysts delight in CBT failures, we might all profit from sharing that excitement in investigating our own failures. It is certainly true that CBT may help someone who has not done well in another form of psychotherapy. It is often the case that withdrawal of multiple medications and an accompanying psychotherapy benefits a patient. Actually these anecdotes should become a clarion cry for further study rather than a condemnation of what has failed. The greatest neglect in our field is that of ignoring what does not seem to work. In a very prophetic statement, Hinshelwood (2003) said, "We have not an ideal model at which we fail sometimes, but a model which has failures at its core" (p. 216). It may well be advisable that all of the many modalities employed to treat mental disorders take this statement to heart. Some things work for some people, and some for others, but all ultimately fail for some. Our allegiances may blind us to those distinctions, and only failure allows us to open our eyes.

THE FILTRATION PROCESS

The businessman is told to "Sell what you make," just as the artisan is advised to "Sell what you do." So, too, do the psychoanalyst and psychotherapist practice their trades. The Lacanian analyst works differently than the Kohutian one, and pretty much everyone practices according to their training and skills. If we follow the path of any patient who seeks some form of psychologic help, we may construct one that consists of a form of a filtration process as an imaginary patient moves through a series of suggested treatments.

Our first patient, whom we shall call Laura, is depressed and goes to her primary care physician, who prescribes an antidepressant. If successful, the procedure goes no further; if a failure, she is referred for a different form of treatment. Laura's friend suggests a psychotherapist, and here one may insist on CBT or a variety of other therapies. Just as with the antidepressant, the filtration process ceases with success. However, a failure usually initiates another form of treatment. Laura is moving down a series of therapeutic interventions, none of which can claim more primacy or significance until or unless they help Laura. Let us now imagine another failure for Laura until she is referred for psychoanalysis. Here, too, we see a variety of possible landing points depending on the particular school and set of beliefs enjoyed and employed by the psychoanalyst. Yet another failure may well lead Laura to but another therapist or analyst. Filtration removes certain possibilities as Laura passes on to others. Each step filters out the failed efforts.

Of course, the imaginary travails of Laura could easily be seen in reverse until she finally, after a succession of psychotherapies, is put on an antidepressant that does the job. There is no necessary and prescribed route leading to success, and it is clear that a failure can present itself at any point in this journey. Success can occur at the beginning or only after a series of failures.

Although the psychoanalyst who Laura last visits may readily make the claim that a majority of his or her patients are "preselected" in that they have passed through a series of evaluations and suggestions before arriving at his or her doorstep, the same may be true of most of the other therapeutic confrontations. Laura has been passing through a filtration process with the hope of a final effective result. It is quite likely that none of her available therapists are aware of exactly where they are situated in this series of steps, inasmuch as another patient may make but a single change, whereas still others may never reach a satisfying endpoint. Some patients pass relentlessly through failure until they reach success, and some surrender without achieving it.

This imaginary filtration process exists in the world of therapy, and it includes all of the extant modalities of treatment from psychotropic medication to group therapy to all of the varieties of psychotherapy and psychoanalysis. Failure characterizes all of them. It exists both within the treatment, as witnessed in both prescribing the wrong medication and experiencing an unanalyzable transference configuration, and outside of the treatment, as seen in the move from a failed psychotherapy to a successful group experience. One can fail in classical psychoanalysis because of an unempathic analyst just as one can fail in Jungian analysis because the narcissistic transference is unrecognized. Therefore at times the failure lies within the intrinsic application of the treatment, whereas at other times it is a case of misapplication and so is extrinsic to the treatment.

The problems with the filtration process are apparent in that clarity is not readily achieved: The drug may help a little, talking to someone does make one feel better, "I really appreciate the support of the group," and so on. The barometers that signal success or failure are either unavailable or ignored. It is unusual to find an analyst who refers a patient for CBT, just as it is rare to find a psychopharmacologist who works closely with a psychoanalyst. These matches do occur, but they remain rare.

Another striking problem with the filtration process is that of the opaqueness of one's position in the series. The suggestion that everyone be placed in psychoanalysis until we discover the factors that allow it to succeed is surely as foolhardy as putting everyone on antidepressants to see what works. One cannot escape the fact that psychoanalysis is quite effective for some, just as CBT is quite effective for some. However, the differences in both the process and the results are enormous, and comparisons based upon simple endpoints are empty.

Just as Laura wished to be relieved of her depression, our second patient, whom we will call Josh, wished to better understand himself. He therefore bypassed a number of available therapies that made no claim to aid in that endeavor. His was a different form of discontent, and so he moved through a different filtration process with a different set of trials and evaluations. However, his journey did seem similar to that of Laura in that there was no clear path to follow when his initial psychotherapy failed, and as he proceeded to one or another form of psychoanalysis. Indeed, most of his therapists or analysts communicated to him that they were the final and correct landing point. The same insularity that Laura found between different forms of treatment seemed to exist between different forms of psychotherapy and psychoanalysis. Kleinian analysts do not refer patients to Jungian analysts, nor do Jungian analysts refer to Kohutians. Sometimes it is a case of disdain for the competition, but often it is simple ignorance of what is offered by others.

A final complication arrives with the explanation. Although (in one fictional narrative) Josh thinks Laura's treatment failed because she did not go to the proper analyst, Laura thinks Josh failed because he should have been medicated. Our imaginary scenarios could also consist of alternate explanations of Josh's conviction that Laura was successful because of her transference to her psychopharmacologist, whereas Laura feels Josh's supposed understanding is a mere make-believe story. Alas, once again failure and success remain elusive. The filtration process cannot do more than describe without certainty. The task for psychiatry and psychoanalysis is not to describe clusters of symptoms but to develop syndromes of treatability.

FINAL THOUGHTS

There can be no doubt that this book is a failure. It has failed at the effort to clearly define failure. The goal of listing the cause or causes of those failures that were considered was never achieved. And certainly in regard to the aim of any helpful direction as to how to either avoid or correct failures, the book was a totally failed exercise. All in all, nothing both substantial and able to be communicated to others was developed and delivered. The answers to these many problems were essentially vague dodges that avoided the central issue. As to definition, the book waffled and said that there was no agreed-upon definition, that the word meant many different things to different people, and that one person's failure might well be another's compromise or even success. And on and on without getting a clear and cogent response. As to causes, there was an abundance of unsettled reasons ranging from ignorance to incompetence to misapplication, but once again it essentially was a smokescreen of imprecision. To add insult to injury, the book ends on a note of expecting others to pursue the very issues that this book failed to fully adequately explain. What a waste.

On the other hand, the book could easily claim to be a success of sorts. It made clear that the term *failure* was not a word that could be definitively defined, because it meant different things at different times to different people. It was based upon a normative scale that was fundamentally a construction of a particular culture at a particular time. Yesteryear's "sick" homosexuality is today's personal preference or orientation. As long as some patients will get better no matter what the form of therapy and no matter who the therapist, *and* some patients will *not* get better no matter who the therapist and no matter what the mode of treatment, then any search for a "cause" is a futile exercise. We can no more pinpoint causes than we can predict results. We can and should, however, get better at matching patient and therapy. Spending a lot of time on merely describing clusters of symptoms and assigning them names and numbers might be a waste, and that energy might be better spent working on the problem of enlarging our vision. That might result in being familiar enough with all of the modes of treatment so that our ultimate goal would be less in the direction of naming disease and more in that of alleviating it.

It is fitting to finish with the insight gained from the patient with whom I began, the one who made me feel a failure. At one point in his analysis, he struggled to unearth the origin and so the explanation of a particular way he viewed a teacher. He insisted that I tell him the answer to his problem, inasmuch as his appraisal of this teacher was clearly irrational and yet something he seemed unable to relinquish and correct. He did liken it to a childhood vision of his father, but he wanted to know exactly why he persisted in this misconception. I myself could come up with all sorts of theoretical explanations from sticky libido to masochism to anxiety about termination, but I honestly did not know the answer to his quandary.

Our analysis of his wish to have his father (and so me) admit to being a failure had not been fully understood, because the complexity of his relationship to his father never allowed us to merely write him off as a failure. There were numerous recollections of the father taking his son (my patient) to do something that turned out to be more than the father could handle. Yet this father always needed reassurance that he was a good father. My own feelings as the patient insisted that I give him an answer was to avoid the feeling of incompetency that was being thrust upon me. Once again, the cloud of failure began to descend upon me until I realized that there need be no good answer to my patient's repeated question. Just as it was ridiculous for the father to take his son sailing when he himself really did not know how to sail well enough, so, too, I needed to recognize that a failure only became such because of a promise. I could still be a good-enough analyst without knowing all the answers. Rather than being a mean father or a bad father or an incompetent father, this patient's father was a limited man who could not live happily with his limitations. But is that not a certain version of failure, not being able to do something because of one or more limitations in spite of one's good intentions? It was only when this father asked his son to reassure him that he had been a good father that he qualified as a failure. Only when I allowed myself to be what my patient wanted did the analysis proceed and succeed.

This book may do no more than be a representative of the "failure" situation. One salient feature of the study of that situation is the resistance to its investigation. Failure is such a dreaded experience that it is regularly ignored, denied, or displaced elsewhere. At the very least, this book may succeed in letting failure come out of the darkness and allowing its presence to be acknowledged. One must live as a failure long enough to allow a personal struggle that in turn may open up a proper objective scrutiny. Feeling a failure should not be merely an impetus to be rid of it, to learn how to avoid it in the future, or to get over it, all perfectly reasonable and worthwhile goals. At long last, it should be an opportunity. The success of the book rests on its embrace of failure.

References

Abend, S. (2000). The problem of therapeutic alliance. In S. T. Levy (Ed.), *The therapeutic alliance* (pp. 1–16). Madison, CT: International Universities Press.

Adler, G. (2000). The alliance and the more disturbed patient. In S. T. Levy (Ed.), *The therapeutic alliance* (pp. 76–77). Madison, CT: International Universities Press.

Agosta, L. (2009). *Empathy in the context of philosophy*. New York: Palgrave Macmillan.

Alexander, F. (1964). Psychoanalysis revised. In *The scope of psychoanalysis* (p. 146). New York: Basic Books (Original work published 1940).

American Psychiatric Association. (2000). *The diagnostic and statistical manual of mental disorders* (4th ed., text rev.). Washington, DC: Author.

American Psychiatric Association. (Forthcoming). *The diagnostic and statistical manual of mental disorders* (5th ed.). Washington, DC: Author.

Araqno, A. (2008). The language of empathy: An analysis of its constitution, development, and role in psychoanalytic listening. *Journal of the American Psychoanalytic Association, 56*, 713–740.

Bacal, H. (1985). Optimal responsiveness and the therapeutic process. In A. Goldberg (Ed.), *Progress in self psychology* (Vol. 1, pp. 202–227). New York: Guilford Press.

Bae, S. C., Hashimoto, H., Karlson, E. W., Liang, M. H., & Daltroy, L. H. (2001). Variable effects of social support by race, economic status, and disease activity in systemic lupus erythematosus. *Journal of Rheumatology, 28*(6), 1245–1251.

Baker, R. (2000). Finding the neutral position. *Journal of the American Psychoanalytic Association, 48*(1), 129–153.

Barlow, D. (2010). Negative effects on psychological treatment: A prospective. *American Psychologist, 68*(1), 18–20.

Basch, M. F. (1983). Empathic understanding: A review of the concept and some theoretical considerations. *Journal of the American Psychoanalytic Association, 31*(1), 101–126.

Bateman, A., & Fonagy, P. (2008). Eight-year follow-up of patients treated for borderline personality disorder: Mentalization-based treatment versus treatment as usual. *American Journal of Psychiatry, 165*, 631–638.

Benjamin, J. (2009). A relational psychoanalysis perspective on the necessity of acknowledging failure in order to restore the facilitating and containing features of the intersubjective relationship (the shared third). *International Journal of Psychoanalysis, 90*, 441–560.

Boston Change Process Study Group (BCPSG). (2008). Forms of relational meaning: Issues in the relations between the implicit and reflective-verbal domains. *Psychoanalytic Dialogues, 18*, 125–148.

Brenner, C. (1955). *An elementary textbook of psychoanalysis.* New York: International Universities Press.

Brenner, C. (1979). Working alliance, therapeutic alliance, and transference. *Journal of the American Psychoanalytic Association, 27*(Suppl.), 137–157.

Brent, D. A., Emslie, G. J., Clarke, G. N., Asarnow, J., Spirito, A., Ritz, L., et al. (2009). Predictors of spontaneous and systematically assessed suicidal adverse events in the treatment of SSRI-resistant depression in adolescents (TORDIA) study. *American Journal of Psychiatry, 166*(4), 418–426.

Brooks, D. (2009, October 13). The young and the neuro. *New York Times*, p. A31.

Cacioppo, J. T., Hawkley, L. C., Crawford, L. E., Ernst, J. M., Burleson, M. H., Kowalewski, R. B., et al. (2002). Loneliness and health: Potential mechanisms. *Psychosomatic Medicine, 64*(3), 407–417.

Caligor, E., Stern, B., Hamilton, M., MacCornack, V., Wininger, L., Sneed, J., & Roose, S. (2009). Why we recommend analytic treatment for some patients and not for others. *Journal of the American Psychoanalytic Association, 57*(3), 677–694.

Carroll, L. (1982). *Through the looking glass.* In *The complete illustrated works of Lewis Carroll* (p. 184). London: Chancellor Press (Original work published 1896).

Carruthers, P. (2009). How we know our own minds: The relationship between mind reading and metacognition. *Behavioral and Brain Science*, *32*, 121–182.

Chessick, R. (1996). Impasse and failure in psychoanalytic treatment. *Journal of the American Academy of Psychoanalysis*, *24*, 193–216.

Collins, S. F. (2003). *The joy of success*. New York: HarperCollins.

Cooper, A. (2008). American psychoanalysis today: A plurality of orthodoxies. *Journal of the American Academy of Psychoanalysis*, *30*(2), 235–253.

Coyne, J. (2009). *Why evolution is true*. New York: Viking.

Delacampagne, C. (1999). *A history of philosophy in the twentieth century*. Baltimore: Johns Hopkins University Press.

Denberg, T. D., Melhado, T. V., Coombes, J. L., Beaty, B. L., & Berman, K. (2005). Predictors of non-adherence to screening colonoscopy. *Journal of General Internal Medicine*, *20*(11), 989–995.

Derrida, J. (1985). *Margins of philosophy* (A. Bass, Trans.). Chicago: University of Chicago Press.

deWaal, F. (2005). *Our inner ape: A leading primatologist explains why we are who we are*. New York: Riverhead Books.

deWaal, F. (2009). *The age of empathy: Nature's lessons for a kinder society*. New York: Harmony.

Doering, S., Horz, S., Rentrop, M., Fischer-Kern, M. (2010). Transference-focused psychotherapy v. Treatment by community psychotherapists for borderline personality disorder: Randomised controlled trial. *The British Journal of Psychiatry* (2010), 196:389–395.

Ellman, S. J. (2010). *When theories touch: A historical and theoretical integration of psychoanalytic thought*. London: Karnac.

Fink, B. (1997). *A clinical introduction to Lacanian psychoanalysis: Theory and technique*. Cambridge, MA: Harvard University Press.

Fink, B. (2010). Against understanding: Why understanding should not be viewed as an essential aim of psychoanalytic treatment. *Journal of the American Psychoanalytic Association*, *58*(2), 259–285.

Firth, C. D., & Wolpert, D. M. (Eds.). (2004). *The neuroscience of social interaction: Decoding, imitating, and influencing the actions of others*. Oxford: Oxford University Press.

Fleming, J., & Benedek, T. (1983). *Psychoanalytic supervision: A method of clinical teaching*. New York: International Universities Press.

Fonagy, P. (1999). Memory and the therapeutic action of psychoanalysis. *International Journal of Psychoanalysis*, *80*, 614–616.

Fonagy, P., Gergely, G., Jurist, E., & Target, M. (2002). *Affect regulation, mentalization, and the development of the self*. New York: Other Press.

Freedman, L. (1969). The therapeutic alliance. *International Journal of Psychoanalysis, 50,* 27–39.

Freud, S. (1925). An autobiographical study. In J. Strachey (Ed. & Trans.), *The standard edition of the complete psychological works of Sigmund Freud* (Vol. 20, pp. 7–76). London: Hogarth Press, 1959.

Freud, S. (1933). New introductory lectures on psychoanalysis. In J. Strachey (Ed. & Trans.), *The standard edition of the complete psychological works of Sigmund Freud* (Vol. 22, pp. 3–182). London: Hogarth Press.

Freud, S. (1957). The dynamics of transference. In J. Strachey (Ed. & Trans.), *The standard edition of the complete psychological works of Sigmund Freud* (Vol. 12, pp. 97–108). London: Hogarth Press (Original work published 1912).

Fried, E. (1954). Self-induced failure: A mechanism of defense. *Psychoanalytic Review, 41,* 330–339.

Gabbard, G. (1994). Psychotherapists who transgress sexual boundaries with patients. *Bulletin of the Menninger Clinic, 58,* 129–135.

Gallese, V. (2008). Empathy, embodied simulation and the brain. *Journal of the American Psychoanalytic Association, 56,* 769–781.

Gedo, J., & Gehrie, M. (Eds.). (1993). *Impasses and innovation in psychoanalysis: Clinical case seminars.* Hillsdale, NJ: Analytic Press.

Gehrie, M. (2009). The evolution of the psychology of the self: Toward a mature narcissism. *Self and Systems, 1159,* 31–50.

Ghaemi, N. (2010, February 26). What's wrong with the biopsychosocial model? Medscape Blogs. Retrieved from http://boards.medscape.com/forums?128@659.8WFJai3BNxL@.29fb1d2e!comment=1

Goldberg, A. (1988). *A fresh look at psychoanalysis.* Hillsdale, NJ: Analytic Press.

Goldberg, A. (1995). *The problem of perversion.* New Haven, CT: Yale University Press.

Goldberg, A. (1999). *Being of two minds: The vertical split in psychoanalysis.* Hillsdale, NJ: Analytic Press.

Goldberg, A. (Ed.). (2000). *Errant selves: A casebook of misbehavior.* Hillsdale, NJ: Analytic Press.

Goldberg, A. (2001). Me and Max: A misalliance of goals. *Psychoanalytic Quarterly, 70,* 117–130.

Goldberg, A. (2004). *Misunderstanding Freud.* New York: Other Press.

Goldberg, A. (2007). *Moral stealth.* Chicago: University of Chicago Press.

Goldberg, A. (2010). On the wish to be invisible. *Psychoanalytic Quarterly, 79,* 381–393.

Grande, T., Dilg, R., Jakobsen, T., Keller, W., Kraweitz, B., Langer, M., et al. (2009). Structural change as a predictor of long-term follow-up outcome. *Psychotherapy Research, 19*(3), 344–357.

Greenson, R. (1978). The working alliance and the transference neurosis. In *Explorations in psychoanalysis* (pp. 199–224). New York: International Universities Press (Original work published 1965).

Hagoort, P., & Levelt, W. (2009). The speaking brain. *Science, 326*(5951), 372–373.

Hawkley, L. G., & Cacioppo, J. T. (2003). Loneliness and pathways to disease. *Brain, Behavior, and Immunity, 17*(Suppl.), 98–105.

Heidegger, M. (1946). *Being and time* (J. Stambough, Trans.). Albany: State University of New York Press. (Original work published 1927)

Hinshelwood, R. D. (2003). What we can learn from failures. In J. Rippen & M. Schulman (Eds.), *Failures in psychoanalytic treatment*. New York: International Universities Press.

Hoch, P. (1948). *Failures in psychiatric treatment*. New York: Grune & Stratton.

Hurley, S. (2008). The shared circuits model: How control, mirroring, and simulation can enable imitation, deliberation, and mind reading. *Behavior and Brain Science, 31*(1), 1–38.

Hyman, M. (2003). In J. Rippen & M. Schulman (Eds.), *Failures in psychoanalytic treatment*. New York: International Universities Press.

Inglis, F. (2009). *History man: The life of R. G. Collingwood*. Princeton, NJ: Princeton University Press.

Janicak, P., Davis, J., Preskorn, S., & Ayd, F. (2006). *Principles and practice of psychopharmacotherapy* (4th ed.). Philadelphia: Lippincott, Williams & Wilkins.

Jurist, E. (2010). Mentalizing minds. *Psychoanalytic Inquiry, 30,* 289–300.

Kantrowitz, J. L. (1993). Impasses in psychoanalysis: Overcoming resistances. *Journal of the American Psychoanalytic Association, 41,* 1021–1050.

Kantrowitz, J. L. (1995). The beneficial aspects of the patient–analyst match. *International Journal of Psychoanalysis, 76,* 299–313.

Kantrowitz, J. L. (1996). Follow-up of psychoanalysis, five to ten years after termination. *Journal of the American Psychoanalytic Association, 38,* 471–496.

Kernberg, O. (1975). *Borderline conditions and pathological narcissism*. New York: Jason Aronson.

Kernberg, O. (1999). Psychoanalysis, psychoanalytic psychotherapy, and supportive psychotherapy: Contemporary controversies. *International Journal of Psychoanalysis, 80,* 1075–1091.

Kohut, H. (1971). *The analysis of the self*. New York: International Universities Press.

Kohut, H. (1977). *The restoration of the self.* New York: International Universities Press.

Kohut, H. (1984). *How does analysis cure?* (A. Goldberg, Ed.). Chicago: University of Chicago Press.

Kuhn, T. (1970), *The Structure of Scientific Revolutions.* University of Chicago Press.

Lazar, S., editor (2010), *Psychotherapy Is Worth It.* Group for the Advancement of Psychiatry. Arlington, VA: American Psychiatric Publishing Inc. Lerner (2009), Minneapolis Star Tribune Website 8/21.

Leichsenring, F., & Robung, S. (2008). Effectiveness of long-term psychodynamic therapy: A meta-analysis. *Journal of the American Medical Association, 3000*(13), 1531–1565.

Lerner, M. "New data show depression's stubborn grasp in Minnesota." August 20, 2009. www.StarTribune.com

Levy, S. T. (2000). *The therapeutic alliance.* Madison, CT: International Universities Press.

Mason, P., & Bartal, I. (2010). How the social brain experiences empathy: Summary of a gathering. *Social Neuroscience, 5*(2), 252–256.

Metzinger, T. (2009). *The ego tunnel.* New York: Basic Books.

Mitchell, S. (1988). *Relational concepts in psychoanalysis.* Cambridge, MA: Harvard University Press.

Mitchell, S. (1995). Interaction in the Kleinian and interpersonal traditions. *Contemporary Psychoanalysis, 31,* 65.

Nahum, J. P. (2002). Explicating the implicit: The local level and the microprocess of change in the analytic situation. *International Journal of Psychoanalysis, 83,* 1031–1062.

Neutzel, E., Larsen, R., & Prizmer, Z. (2007). The dynamics of empirically derived factors in the therapeutic relationship. *Journal of the American Psychoanalytic Association, 55*(4), 1321–1353.

New York Times, March 20, 2010, p. A9.

Ogden, T. (1982). Treatment of the schizophrenic state of non-experience. In L. B. Boyer & P. L. Giovacchini (Eds.), *Technical factors in the treatment of the severely disturbed patient.* New York: Jason Aronson.

Okrent, A. (2009). *In the land of invented languages.* New York: Spiegel & Grau.

Paolino, T. (1981). Analyzability: Some categories for assessment. *Contemporary Psychoanalysis, 17*(3), 321–340.

Parkes, C. M., & Stevenson-Hinde, J. (Eds.). (1982). *The place of attachment in human behavior.* New York: Basic Books.

Renik, O. (2000). Discussion of the Therapeutic Alliance. In S. T. Levy (Ed.), *The therapeutic alliance*. Madison, CT: International Universities Press.

Ricoeur, P. (1992). *Oneself as another*. Chicago: University of Chicago Press.

Rippen, J., & Schulman, M. (2003). *Failures in psychoanalytic treatment*. Madison, CT: International Universities Press.

Robbins, F., & Schlessinger, N. (1983). *Developmental view of the psychoanalytic process: Follow-up studies and their consequences*. Madison, CT: International Universities Press.

Rosenblatt, A. (2010). The place of long-term and intensive psychotherapy. In S. G. Lazar (Ed.), *Psychotherapy is worth it: A comprehensive view of its cost-effectiveness* (pp. 289–310). Arlington, VA: American Psychiatric Publishing.

Rosenblum, S. (1994). Report of a panel on analyzing the "unanalyzable" patient: Implications for technique. *Journal of the American Psychoanalytic Association, 42*(4), 1251–1259.

Rudolf, J., Grande, T., Dilg, R., Jakobsen, T., Keller, W., Oberbracht, C., et al. (2002). Structural changes in psychoanalytic therapies: The Heidelberg-Berlin study on long-term psychoanalytic therapies (PAL). In M. Leuzinger-Bohleber & M. Target (Eds.), *Longer term psychoanalytic treatment: Perspectives for therapists and researchers* (pp.). London: Whurr.

Ruti, M. (2008). The fall of fantasies: A Lacanian reading of lack. *Journal of the American Psychoanalytic Association, 56*(2), 483–508.

Schafer, R. (1968). *Aspects of internalization*. Madison, CT: International Universities Press.

Schafer, R. (1992). *Retelling a life: Narration and dialogue in psychoanalysis*. New York: Basic Books.

Schwartz, B., & Flowers, J. V. (2010). *How to fail as a therapist: 50 ways to lose or damage your patients*. Atascadoro, CA: Impact.

Shedler, J. (2010). The efficacy of psychodynamic psychotherapy. *American Psychologist, 65*(2), 98–109.

Socarides, C. (1995). *Homosexuality: A freedom too far*. New York: Roberkai.

Stepansky, P. (2009). *Psychoanalysis at the margins*. New York: Other Press.

Summers, F. (2008). Theoretical insularity and the crisis of psychoanalysis. *Psychoanalytic Psychology, 23*(3), 413–424.

Thompson, J. J. (2010). *Normativity*. Chicago: Open Court.

Van Anders, S. M., & Watson, N. (2007). Testosterone levels in women and men who are single, in long-distance relationships, or same-city relationships. *Hormones and Behavior, 51*(2), 286–291.

Vida, J. (2003). In J. Rippen & M. Schulman (Eds.), *Failures in psychoanalytic treatment*. New York: International Universities Press.

Vivona, J. M. (2009). Leaping from brain to mind: A critique of mirror neuron explanations of countertransference. *Journal of the American Psychoanalytic Association, 57*, 525–550.

Wallerstein, R. S. (1966). The current state of psychotherapy. *Journal of the American Medical Association, 14*, 183–244.

Wallerstein, R. S. (1986). *Forty-two lives in treatment*. New York: Guilford Press.

Wallerstein, R. S., & Coen, S. J. (1994). Impasse in psychoanalysis. *Journal of the American Psychoanalytic Association, 42*, 1225–1235.

Wanderer, J. (2008), *Robert Brandon, Philosophy Now*. Montreal and Kingston, Ithaca: McGill-Queens University Press, p. 171.

Wispe, L. (1987). History of the concept of empathy. In N. Eisenberg & J. Strayer (Eds.), *Empathy and its development* (pp. 17–37). Cambridge: Cambridge University Press.

Wolman, B. J. (1972). *Success and failure in psychoanalysis and psychotherapy*. New York: Macmillan.

Wood, D. (2002). *Thinking after Heidegger*. Cambridge: Polity Press.

Zetzel, E. (1966). The analytic situation. In R. E. Litman (Ed.), *Psychoanalysis in the Americas* (pp. 86–106). New York: International Universities Press.

Index